D0849165

FOREIGN DIRECT INVESTMENT
in the
UNITED STATES
Issues, Magnitudes, and Location Choice
of New Manufacturing Plants

Jan Ondrich
Michael Wasylenko
Syracuse University

1993

W.E. UPJOHN INSTITUTE for Employment Research
Kalamazoo, Michigan

Library of Congress Cataloging-in-Publication Data

Ondrich, Jan, 1954-
    Foreign direct investment in the United States : issues,
magnitudes, and location choice of new manufacturing plants / Jan Ondrich
and Michael Wasylenko.
        p. cm.
    Includes bibliographical references and index.
    ISBN 0-88099-140-2 (cloth). — ISBN 0-88099-139-9 (pbk.)
    1. United States—Manufactures—Foreign ownership.   2. United
States—Manufactures—Location.   3. United States—Industries—
Foreign ownership.   4. United States—Industries—Location.
United States.   7. Labor market—United States.   8. Balance of
payments—United States.   I. Wasylenko, Michael J.   II. Title.
HD9725.053   1993
332.6'73'0973—dc20   93-23240
                                                                                          CIP

$HD9725$
$.053$
1993

Copyright © 1993
W.E. Upjohn Institute for Employment Research
300 S. Westnedge Avenue
Kalamazoo, Michigan 49007-4686

Cover design by J.R. Underhill.
Index prepared by Shirley Kessel.
Printed in the United States of America.

Acknowledgments

During the course of our research on this monograph, we have accumulated many deficit positions ourselves. We wish to acknowledge our debts to many people, although that by itself will not eliminate the debt.

We are grateful to the W. E. Upjohn Institute for Employment Research for supporting our research. Timothy Bartik of the Institute, our colleague Douglas Holtz-Eakin, and two anonymous referees made many useful comments on earlier drafts of this work. We thank them for their ideas and for their conscientious efforts to improve our work. Still, we could not incorporate all of their ideas, and the remaining shortcomings of our work are our doing.

In earlier stages of the work Robert Carroll, now at the Department of Treasury and Jingyu Oh of the Korea Energy Economics Institute delivered high-quality research assistance. Their work is present in many aspects of this book.

In addition, several staff members of the Metropolitan Studies Program of the Maxwell School at Syracuse University improved mightily on the presentation of our work. Esther Gray typed many drafts of chapters and made suggestions for improvement in presentation of tables and manuscript style. Karin D'Agostino worked on our maps and graphics to transform our crude ideas to first-rate representations of our findings. Laura Griffin made many editorial improvements throughout the manuscript and typed several drafts of the chapters as well. We owe a substantial debt of gratitude to these friends.

Our families also managed to ignore us when we were distracted by yet another setback. Mia Ondrich, however, contributed in substantial ways to our analysis. We thank Mia and Laura Ondrich and Lydia and Thomas Wasylenko for their patience and indulgence.

The Authors

Jan Ondrich is Associate Professor of Economics and Senior Research Associate of the Metropolitan Studies Program, Maxwell School of Citizenship and Public Affairs, at Syracuse University.

Michael Wasylenko is Professor and Chair of the Economics Department at Syracuse University and Associate Director of the Metropolitan Studies Program.

Contents

List of Tables

List of Figures

FOREIGN DIRECT INVESTMENT
in the
UNITED STATES

1
Introduction

Foreign investment has become a major focus for Americans. It was an issue during the 1988 and 1992 Presidential races, and some policy-makers believe that there is a link between more foreign investment in the United States and the growth of our federal government budget deficits. In particular, foreign investment inflows balance the deficit in our export-import account, which could result from a lack of private and government saving or government deficits.

Some Americans have even come to view foreign investment in the United States negatively. In a recent appearance in the then Federal Republic of Germany, Bob Hope joked to his audience of United States military personnel, "You remember back home, that's the country you are protecting for the Japanese *(investors)."* While the remark drew much laughter, it also suggests that most people misunderstand the extent to which foreign investors own our country, exactly what they own, who the investors are, and what benefits might be associated with foreign investment.

Foreign portfolio and direct investments in the United States have increased dramatically during the past two decades.[1] By 1989 for example, expenditures on new plants and equipment by foreign firms located in the United States accounted for 12.3 percent of total nonresidential gross private investment in the United States and the percentage grew steadily throughout the 1980s (Bezirganian 1991). Such trends have caused alarm in some quarters, because the earnings on capital in the United States will increasingly accrue to persons living outside of the United States.

On the other hand, direct foreign investment creates jobs, about 4.4 million jobs as of 1989. In 1989, 4.8 percent of the United States work-force were employed by a foreign-held firm, and 9.3 percent of the manufacturing workforce were employed by a foreign-held firm (Bezirganian 1991).

In addition, aggregate saving for use in financing domestic investment in the United States is low, and foreign investment augments our capital stock and enhances the productivity of our workforce. Not only may additional capital raise productivity and real wages of workers, but the new capital may embody technological advances that compound the effect of added capital on our economic growth. Moreover, foreign plants have brought to the workplace new management practices which, in many cases, have arguably heightened worker satisfaction and efficiency. Thus, it could be said that foreign investment has spared our nation from an otherwise more dire employment picture and national recession. If there is a problem with foreign investment being an increasing share of our total investment, the problem might be better cast as our investing too little in our physical capital rather than foreigners investing too much.

While a broad overview may belie the title of this book, we believe that a thorough understanding of what foreign investment is and the theory that surrounds its origins is necessary to understand the implications of foreign investment for a nation or a state. Ultimately, however, we want to help state policymakers understand what drives the location choices of foreign plants. Our findings may help states shape, refocus, and refine their recruitment strategies for foreign plants.

A number of studies of foreign plant locations exist. We augment the evidence by using a larger data set spanning many more years and by experimenting with more general and efficient econometric techniques. In examining the factors that influence the state location decisions of new foreign plants, we use a pooled cross-section and time-series data set for states of individual manufacturing plant location choices for the period 1978 to 1987.[2] In the end, we are not as convinced as others seem to be that certain aspects of state and local taxation and spending significantly influence foreign plant location decisions.

The difficulty of modeling the taxation of foreign corporations should not be underestimated, however. As we show in more detail later in this chapter, the taxation of companies in general, and of multinational companies in particular, is so complex that making *a priori* predictions about the effects of tax policy is heroic indeed. We emphasize that in a domestic corporate setting it seems generally safe to argue that specific changes in tax policy will likely have the expected incentive effects on whatever behavior is being modeled, other things equal. However, in the case of multinational companies, the system of intercountry tax credits and treaties and the opportunities to avoid taxation may make it difficult to understand whether a specific tax action in a country indeed raises taxes to multinational corporations located within its borders.

We have two main objectives in this chapter. First, we elaborate on the broader economic and taxation issues that surround foreign direct investment. Beginning with the definitions of foreign direct investment, we then explain inward (foreign investments in the United States) and outward (U.S. investments outside the United States) trends in foreign investment over time. The discussion turns to an examination of economic theories of foreign investment, or why investors produce in other countries. We then examine the economic implications of our debtor nation status for investment and growth in the United States.

Armed with this overview of aggregate investment trends and their implications, we turn to how taxation might affect foreign investment at both the national and the state and local levels. In that context, we discuss "economically efficient" taxation of international capital before we introduce the complexities of actual tax laws as they apply to multinational corporations.

A second objective of the chapter is to introduce the location data used to examine the foreign direct investment trends in various states and industries within the United States. Here, we present the types of foreign direct investments by year and the number of new manufacturing plants by industry group and by country of the major investor.

The Larger Setting

An understanding of the broad picture surrounding foreign investment is useful in making policy recommendations to states about attracting foreign direct investment (FDI). Knowledge of the significance of FDI in our economy, whether national policies thwart FDI, and how FDI affects our national well-being should all play a role in the design of state policies to attract FDI. In this section of the chapter, we focus on the broad implications of FDI to deepen the understanding of our FDI location results and the policy recommendations that may flow from them.

Definitions of Foreign Investment

At an aggregate level, foreign investment includes both portfolio and direct investment. Portfolio assets are stocks, bonds, and other private and government-held securities. FDI, however, does not correspond to investment in plant and equipment as we know it. An awareness of the differences between the definition of FDI and more common National Income and Product Account definitions of investment in plant and equipment will illuminate some of the results presented in the empirical literature.[3]

FDI is measured as earnings retained by subsidiaries or branches in the United States and transfers of funds from parent firms to their foreign subsidiaries in the United States. The transfers include both debt and equity raised capital. The measurement of FDI, therefore, omits the investment made by the foreign subsidiaries when the capital is borrowed either within the host country or in a third country. In addition, aggregate FDI includes purchases of existing companies and real estate transactions. The latter transactions are better described as a transfer of assets rather than as new investments in plant and equipment. FDI then is actually a measure of the financial flow of assets. Similarly, when the term "foreign investment position" is used, it should be understood to mean the financial stock of assets held by foreigners, which includes purchases of existing assets but omits investment financed from the subsidiaries' borrowed funds.[4]

In addition to the above definitional problems with the measure, the U.S. Department of Commerce has measured until recently both inward and outward FDI based on the book value of the assets. Thus, it failed to revalue the FDI assets to account for inflation and depreciation as discussed in Slemrod (1989) and Glickman and Woodward (1989). The historical or book-value measure of the stocks of FDI in countries likely underestimates the value of U.S. outward investment (investment abroad) relatively more than inward investment of other countries in the United States, as many of the investments of U.S. firms were made longer ago than the more recent investments in the United States by the Japanese and several other countries.

Recently, however, the U.S. Department of Commerce has measured the current-cost and market values of U.S. aggregate inward and outward FDI flows.[5] The agency also retrospectively converted the aggregate measures of historical or book-value data since 1982 to current-cost and market values. But disaggregated FDI flows by country or by industry are at this time only available on historical or book-value bases.

Another issue in measuring FDI is that the value of foreign investment is converted to U.S. dollars using exchange rates between countries, and exchange rate fluctuations can bring large and sometimes temporary swings in the measures of investment values. Using the more stable, but also controversial, purchasing power parity measure to convert investment from foreign currencies to U.S. dollars could also change the relative investment standing of the United States vis-a-vis its inward investors.[6]

Despite the above-mentioned limitations of the data, it is clear by any method of measurement that inward investment in the United States has accelerated and U.S. outward investment has decelerated, especially in the 1980s. We examine the aggregate trends in U.S. inward and outward foreign investment below.

Aggregate Trends in Foreign Investment

Portfolio assets—stocks, bonds, private and government securities—dominate the U.S. holdings by foreign investors, accounting for 79 percent of their total (portfolio plus direct) cumulative assets evaluated on a current-cost basis in 1991. FDI, defined as investment in real estate and investment in industry, accounts for 21 percent of foreigners' total cumulative U.S. asset holdings in 1991 evaluated on a current-cost basis (see table 1.1). While the stock of FDI has decreased as a percentage of the total foreign capital stock since 1982, when it was 24 percent of the total inward foreign investment position, FDI stock evaluated on a current-cost basis in the United States still grew at a 14 percent annual rate between 1982 and 1991.[7]

In fact, the rapid increase in inward foreign investment in the United States put the net overall investment position of the United States into deficit on a current-cost basis in 1987. Moreover, the deficit on a current-cost basis increased steadily thereafter and reached $362 billion

**Table 1.1 Foreign Investment Position in the United States and U.S.
Investment Abroad: Historical, Current-Cost and Market
Value, 1982, 1986, 1990, 1991**

	1982	1986	1990	1991
Total United States Investment Abroad (outflow positions)				
Historical	939,691	1,248,883	1,684,698	1,755,237
Current Cost	1,1 19,178	1,410,190	1,884,199	1,960,301
Market Value	958,577	1,507,734	1,977,053	2,107,041
United States Direct Investment Abroad				
Historical	207, 752	259,860	424,086	450,196
Current Cost	387,239	421,167	623,587	655,260
Market Value	226,638	518,711	716,441	802,000
United States Portfolio Investment Abroad	731,939	989,023	1,260,612	1,305,041
Total Investment in the United States (inflow position)				
Historical	688,052	1,34 6,036	2,109,222	2,242,359
Current Cost	740,245	1,391,455	2,179,035	2,321,804
Market Value	693,803	1,398,588	2,249,080	2,488,876
Direct Investment in the United States				
Historical	124,677	220,414	396,702	407,577
Current Cost	176,870	265,833	466,515	487,022
Market Value	130,428	272,966	536, 560	654,094
Portfolio Investment in the United States	563,375	1,125,622	1,712,520	1,834,782
Net Total Investment (outflow less inflow)				
Historical	251,639	(97,153)	(424,524)	(487,122)
Current Cost	378,933	18,735	(294,836)	(361,503)
Market Value	264,774	109,146	(272,027)	(381,835)
Net Direct Investment Position				
Historical	83, 075	39,446	27,384	42,619
Current Cost	210,369	155,334	157,072	168,238
Market Value	96,210	245,745	179,881	147,906
Net Portfolio Investment	168,564	(136,599)	(451,908)	(529,741)

SOURCE: Scholl, Mataloni, and Bezirganian (1992).

by 1991 (see table 1.1). The net positions of portfolio and direct investments are quite different, however. The U.S. net position of portfolio
investment became negative in 1985 and has ballooned to over half a
trillion dollars by 1991. By contrast, the United States maintained a
surplus position in FDI of $168 billion on a current-cost basis. None-
theless, inflows of FDI have exceeded outflows during most years in
the 1980s and the U.S. net surplus position in FDI has been shrinking
(see figure 1.1).

Panel A of table 1.2 lists the FDI asset values (excluding portfolio)
in the United States by country of the investor. In 1991, investors in the
United Kingdom, Japan, the Netherlands, and Canada held 70 percent
of the FDI asset values in the United States (see table 1.2 Panel B). As
a percent of total direct foreign asset value, the United Kingdom's
share has increased from about 23 percent of the total in 1982 to 26
percent of the total in 1991. During the same nine-year period, Japanese investors increased their share of total FDI stock in the U.S. from
8 to 21 percent. In contrast, the shares held by Canada, the Netherlands, and the group of all other countries have fallen during the 1982
to 1991 period.

As shown in Panel C of table 1.2, the inward total foreign direct
investment asset value in the United States grew at a 14 percent annual
rate during the 1982 to 1991 period. Japanese investors led the growth
with a 28 percent annual increase, while United Kingdom asset values
grew at a 16 percent annual rate. The asset values of Canada, the Netherlands, and the aggregate of other countries grew less rapidly than
those of the United Kingdom and Japan, but still the former group
averaged annual growth rates between 10 and 11 percent during the
1982 to 1991 period.

The rapid inflows of FDI to the United States in the 1980s have
decelerated significantly, however. Between 1990 and 1991, FDI assets
in the United States increased by less than 3 percent, with Canada and
the Netherlands not increasing their book value of FDI in the United
States. The values for the United Kingdom, Japan, and all other countries also slowed down considerably compared to their growth rates in
the 1980s. The recession in the United States, as well as slower real
income growth worldwide, probably contributed to the slowdown in
U.S. inward FDI.

Figure 1.1 Net Investment of the United States

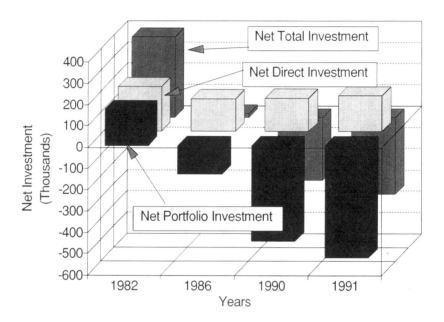

To summarize, investors from four countries make most of the inward foreign investment in the United States. States that actively seek foreign investment might usefully focus their efforts on these four countries. Nonetheless, the rate of increase in inward investment from all four countries has decreased since 1990 compared to the rates of increase during the 1980s. While states are probably less likely to find foreign investors in the 1990s than in the 1980s, they may still have a higher probability of attracting investments from the heavily investing countries of Japan and the United Kingdom than from other countries.

Table 1.2 Foreign Direct Investment Position in the United States, by Country of the Major Investors, 1982, 1986, 1990, 1991 (based on historical values)

Year	Total	Canada	United Kingdom	Netherlands	Japan	Other
Panel A (in millions of dollars)						
1982	124,677	11,708	28,447	26,19	19,677	48,654
1986	220,414	20,318	55,935	40,717	26,824	76,620
1990	396,702	30,037	102,790	63,938	81,775	118,162
1991	407,577	30,002	106,064	63,848	86,658	121,005
Panel B (as a percent of total)						
1982	100.0	9.4	22.8	21.0	7.8	39.0
1986	100.0	9.22	5.41	8.51	2.2	34.8
1990	100.0	7.6	25.9	16.1	20.6	29.8
1991	100.0	7.4	26.0	15.7	21.3	29.7
Panel C (annual percentage growth rates)						
1982 to 1991	14.1	11.0	15.7	10.4	27.5	10.6
1982 to 1986	15.3	14.8	18.4	11.7	29.0	12.0
1986 to 1990	15.8	10.3	16.4	11.9	32.1	11.4
1990 to 1991	2.7	-0.1	3.2	-0.1	6.0	2.4

Sources: Scholl, Mataloni, and Bezirganian (1992), U.S. Department of Commerce (1988), Chung and Fouch (1983).

Rationales for Investing in Foreign Countries

Why invest in other countries? To address this issue, it is useful to distinguish between portfolio and direct investment, as the motivations for each type of investment differ. Portfolio investment is motivated by differentials in the return to capital between countries and by diversification of investors' portfolios. Tax considerations, exchange rate risk, and other factors that affect the return to capital will enter investors' decisions about where (in which countries) to invest.

Cost of capital might also drive decisions about direct investment in other countries. But industrial organization motivations may also explain FDI. Given the competing theories explaining FDI, we turn to a fuller discussion of the motivations for FDI.

In a smooth neoclassical world, for example, factors and goods would flow freely among countries and leave little scope for direct investment. But sustained differentials among countries in the cost of capital could induce FDI, because lower capital costs in some countries will reduce production costs and create competitive advantages.

Graham and Krugman (1991) note that more sophisticated cost-of-capital theories might explain some of the investment flows. For example, foreign investors might discount long-term corporate profit flows at lower real interest rates and thus value a U.S. firm more highly than a domestic investor would. A second capital-cost theory begins with foreign corporations generating higher profits than domestic firms. Then, if internally generated funds are viewed as less costly than raising equity or borrowing, foreign firms with cash will have a lower cost of capital for investment than domestic firms, while domestic firms with lower earnings might have to finance the investment using higher-cost equity or borrowing instruments.

In addition, tax differentials among countries could also cause variation in the marginal effective returns to direct investments among investors from different countries. Due to the complexities involved in the taxation of international capital, however, perceived differentials in tax rates will not necessarily translate directly to different marginal effective tax rates among countries. International tax aspects of capital are discussed in more detail in a subsequent section of this chapter.

A troublesome point, however, with the differential cost-of-capital explanation of FDI is that differentials in the cost of capital among countries explain one-way but not the two-way flows of capital that are commonly observed between countries. Some economists, therefore, have suggested that imperfect competition and industrial organization considerations rather than the cost of capital explain FDI flows among countries. In fact, industrial organization theories of foreign direct investment have competed with the cost-of-capital approach for some time (Hymer 1976). Industrial organization explanations rely on competitive advantages inherent in the technology, the management, the organization of labor, and the vertical integration of key suppliers of intermediate inputs to the finished product as primary explanations of foreign direct investment. In effect, an imperfect market for information about production and organization and first-mover advantages into markets with products that have increasing returns to scale cost structures give some firms a competitive advantage that may last for a considerable period of time. The advantage means the foreign firms will outbid domestic firms for land and plants in an industry.

For some time, it seems U.S. firms enjoyed a competitive advantage over foreign firms, and U.S. firms invested heavily overseas. Recently, the competitive advantage in some industries may have shifted to firms headquartered in certain other countries, and those firms have invested heavily in the United States.

Added to the inherent competitive advantages that underlie much of the industrial organization theory of foreign firms' investment in certain industries may be a layer of U.S. tariffs or quotas aimed at protecting domestic firms from international trade in these same industries. Ironically, the tariffs or quotas give foreign firms with competitive advantages further incentive to invest in the United States to exploit the competitive advantage and to circumvent the tariff or quota.

How Mobile is Foreign Capital?

Attracting foreign investors could be viewed as a bright spot in our economy. The fact that foreigners invest in the United States as well as at home means that they are optimistic about the long-term prospects for the United States economy. Foreign investment might promote productivity increases without increased domestic saving. The productivity increase will lead to higher real wages for workers in the United States, although foreign ownership of capital means that the capital earnings will accrue to persons external to the United States. With foreign investment fueling our productivity surge, we will begin to become a nation of workers and not capitalists.

For some time, however, economists have thought that there is an important link between the amount of domestic saving in an economy and the amount of total investment in the economy. The explicit link between domestic saving and investment leaves little room for foreign investment to play a significant investment role in the economic growth of a country. The linkage between domestic saving and investment not only relegates foreign investment to a minor role in the economy, it also suggests that capital is relatively immobile among countries. Overall, if capital is immobile across countries, the large inward flow of capital to the United States during the 1980s may be an aberration and may not be available in the future for sustaining our economic growth. More to the point of this study, if capital is immobile, states may find foreign investment less available and more difficult to attract in future years.

A long list of studies beginning with Feldstein and Horioka (1980) have examined the extent of international capital flows or the strength in the linkage between domestic saving and investment. Feldstein and Horioka (1980) list three reasons why international capital may not flow perfectly among countries, and why domestic saving tends to be invested in the home country for investment. First, there are additional uncertainties and risks associated with investments in other countries, such as exchange rate risk when large liabilities or profits are denominated in dollars. Second, investors may be wary of existing or future export controls imposed by the host countries or increases in host country tax policy on foreign investment. Finally, there are institutional rigidities in countries that hinder foreign investment. Feldstein and Horioka indeed found evidence that domestic saving and aggregate investment were strongly related, or implicitly that international capital was relatively immobile in their sample of 21 Organization for Economic Cooperation and Development (OECD) countries during the 1960 to 1974 period.

Several other researchers have extended the Feldstein and Horioka results to other countries and tested the hypothesis using data for more recent years. Dooley, Frankel, and Mathieson (1987) examined the saving-investment link in 14 industrialized countries and 48 developing countries. Reasoning that exchange rates may affect capital mobility, they tested their model for the Bretton Woods era of fixed exchange rates, 1960 to 1973, and the post-Bretton Woods era from 1974 to 1984. They also found a statistically robust relationship between domestic saving and aggregate investment in both exchange rate regimes.

Even so, large current account (export minus import) imbalances in many countries during the 1980s require counterbalancing capital flows among countries. That being the case, the empirical findings that domestic saving is the strongest and almost the exclusive predictor of investment in a country are inconsistent with the counterbalancing capital flows predicted by theory. Obstfeld (1986) and other critics attempt to resolve the inconsistency by arguing that spurious correlation exists between domestic saving and investment, and that the Feldstein-Horioka results are based on spurious correlation and therefore incorrect. The spurious correlation between saving and investment could result, for example, when saving and investment are in fact related to a common variable, such as Gross Domestic Product.

Responding to the spurious correlation criticism, Feldstein and Bacchetta (1991) have recently updated the Feldstein and Horioka work by re-estimating the models to account for the possibility of spurious correlation and by using data covering the 1960 through 1986 period.[8] While the general result remains that savings tend to stay at home, their results from the 1980s reveal a somewhat weakened link between domestic saving and aggregate investment. In addition, Feldstein and Bacchetta find that capital moves more freely among the countries in the European Economic Community with their strong economic linkages than it does among nations in the rest of the world. Nonetheless, the findings suggest an unusually strong link between domestic saving and aggregate investment; the link is certainly much stronger than would be expected in a perfectly integrated capital market.

Empirical findings of domestic saving determining investment give rise to theories about and tests of capital market integration or the degree of capital mobility among countries (Frankel 1992). Given that there are saving and investment imbalances and current account imbalances among countries, imperfect capital mobility among countries would mean that the real returns to capital differ among countries. Put another way, when domestic saving and investment imbalances exist among countries, perfect capital mobility among countries could lead to equal (covered) real returns to capital among countries.

For example, Frankel suggests that real returns to capital measured in terms of covered-interest rates should be equal among countries if capital is perfectly mobile among countries. Covered-interest parity accounts for differences in real interest rates among countries, for expected changes in real interest rates, for expected changes in real exchange rates between the currencies, and for a risk premium for real exchange rate risk.[9] The evidence shows that covered-interest rate differentials between the United States and other countries are at or very near zero during each year of the 1974 to 1992 period. Put more directly, the evidence suggests that capital markets are operating near perfectly to equalize covered-interest rates. That evidence casts doubt on the Feldstein-Horioka results. However, Frankel also notes that the United Kingdom and Japan as recently as 1979, and France and Italy as recently as 1986, had capital controls and other barriers to the movement of their capital to other nations. Nonetheless, the movement of capital seems less restricted now in the absence of the financial controls, even if the controls once dampened world capital movements. The evidence at present points to significant international capital mobility and to a potentially significant role for foreign capital in the economic growth of nations.

Direct Taxation and Foreign Investment: Principles and Practice

Given a significant degree of, if not perfect, capital mobility, capital movements and direct investment may be expected to respond to tax differentials among countries. While foreign investors are unlikely to base their investment decision solely on taxation, especially in light of the role of industrial organization considerations in the investment decision, taxation can in some cases play a decisive role in the location of the investment. If, for example, investors have already decided to invest abroad, then federal, state, and local taxation policies can influence where they invest and whether they raise the investment funds through debt or equity. The research reported in this volume concerns, in part, the role that state fiscal policy plays in the location of FDI within the United States.

Before we describe the taxation of foreign investors, it is useful to describe the normative implications of several tax positions that business leaders or policymakers take in regard to the taxation of international capital. To that end we begin with a normative discussion of the economic welfare implications of typical tax regimes that are applied toward foreign investors, because different tax regimes can raise or lower output in the world or in a country. We then focus more specifically on the tax systems that apply to major foreign investors in the United States.

Economic Welfare Implications of Tax Regimes Applied to Foreign Investors

A tax principle that economic policymakers and business people often advocate is a "level playing field." However, that term often has a different meaning for economists than for business people. Economists approach tax policy from an economic welfare perspective or the efficient allocation of capital, which implies maximizing output and, thus, the return to capital. However, output maximization can be done from a worldwide viewpoint or from a single-nation viewpoint. Those with a world view of output maximization would start with the notion that taxation should not distort the allocation of capital investment across countries, nor should it reduce the level of overall investment in the world. That being the case, maximizing world economic welfare means that managers make the same location and investment decisions with a tax system as they would in the absence of a tax system.

Worldwide Neutrality

Tax systems designed to achieve the maximization of world output and return to capital are referred to as "capital-export neutral" (CEN). Using a residence-based tax system, the home country generally taxes foreign income at home country rates and grants a tax credit for taxes paid in the host country. In many cases, the home country imposes taxes on foreign income only when it is repatriated to the home country (with deferral).

To achieve CEN, tax policy designers would insure that the marginal effective tax rates are zero both for international investments (or exported capital) and for home country investments. Capital income would still be taxed; a positive amount of tax would be paid on economic rents (returns above the marginal or normal rate of return) earned on inframarginal capital investments. To the extent that economic rents on capital differ among countries, average tax rates on inframarginal capital would still vary among investments within the home country and between investments in the home and the host countries (Caves 1982).

To reach a zero marginal effective tax rate and a completely neutral tax system for capital, for example, McLure (1992) proposes using a consumption-based corporate income tax. Using a residence-based tax system, the home country would tax corporate income earned in a foreign country (without deferral) and grant credits to foreign firms against home country tax liabilities for taxes paid to foreign governments. A zero effective marginal tax rate occurs if investment in plant and equipment in foreign operations as well as in domestic operations is expensed against corporate income rather than depreciated. Investment expensing or immediate write-off of foreign and domestic investment implies an efficient allocation of capital across countries as well as an efficient level of investment.[10]

Two other tax methods would achieve CEN in the allocation of capital across countries; however, because the marginal effective tax rate is not zero, each method reduces the level of investment in the world. One approach exempts capital from taxation in the host country, while the home country would tax the capital income. In this case, the need for the tax credit in the home country for foreign taxes paid is eliminated. As capital income is not taxed by host countries, capital investment at home and abroad is taxed at the same rate, or CEN is achieved. Under a second tax method, the home country taxes corporate affiliates in other countries (with no income deferral) but allows a full tax credit for taxes paid to the host country. Both tax methods would neutralize taxation as a determinant of location; however, without investment expensing neither guarantees that the marginal effective tax rates are zero. A nonzero marginal tax rate depresses the level of world investment even if the tax system does not affect the relative location of capital investment.

A National Focus for Maximization

National policymakers are more typically concerned with maximizing national income (private income plus government revenue) from capital rather than worldwide income from capital. In this scenario, when marginal effective tax rates are greater than zero, policymakers would implement tax policy designed to keep capital at home until its gross return (including taxes) at home equaled its after-tax return in other countries. Under those conditions, the home country's income maximization would include the sum of the private returns to investors and the home government's revenue. To achieve national income maximization, foreign taxes paid are deducted from the firm's total foreign income and the home country tax rate is applied to the capital income net of foreign taxes.[11] (Figure 1.2 contains a summary of the economic welfare effects of residence-based tax systems.)

A Third Viewpoint

Business leaders hold a third view of a "level playing field." They consider neither worldwide nor national capital income maximization principles. Instead, they generally feel that "foreign plants" operating in the United States, for example, should pay the same tax rate as domestic plants operating in the United States. Foreign operations paying lower taxes than domestic plants are viewed as receiving a subsidy compared to counterpart domestic plants. That being the case, business leaders would favor territorial tax systems, under which the foreign investors pay the taxes of the host country with no home country taxation of foreign capital. Such a system is known as "capital-import neutral," as foreigners investing in the host country pay the same tax rates as domestic investors. A territorial tax system has no particular normative economic welfare implications. However, territorial tax systems can be "capital-export neutral," if the marginal effective tax rates are uniform across countries, or, for example, if all countries operate a territorial tax system and allow the expensing of investment in plant and equipment in the calculation of taxable income.

Figure 1.2   Economic Implications of Hypothetical Residence-Based Tax Systems

	Influences the location of capital	Depresses the level of investment	Maximizes national income for capital	Maximizes world income from capital
Foreign investors pay home country tax rate with a credit for foreign taxes paid and:				
Investment at home and abroad is expensed	No	No	No	Yes
Investment at home and abroad is not expensed	No	Yes	No	No
Foreign investors pay home country tax rate with a deduction for taxes paid in the host country	Yes	Yes	Yes	No

Breaking the Molds

Hufbauer (1992) suggests an alternative to the traditional thinking about the influence of taxation on the mobility of capital across countries. He notes, as discussed above, that modern international trade theory places industrial-organization reasons ahead of tax policies as a motivation for multinational investment decisions. Stated in its pure form, imperfectly competitive firms choose locations based purely on market advantages. Location decisions based on industrial-organization considerations would significantly blunt the welfare implications of CEN as direct foreign investment is not responsive to taxation.[12]

Hufbauer's view of the motivations for the investment decisions of multinational firms allows him to argue for a territorial tax system in which the United States, for example, develops tax policies designed to capture a greater share of desirable foreign investments. He suggests that corporate tax credits for a generous portion of research and development expenses for both domestic and foreign firms might induce more high-technology firms, which tend to pay higher wages, to expand in the United States.[13] Such a tax system, however, might stir international competition in tax systems to attract firms. Nonetheless, given that business generally favors a territorial tax system, domestic business competitors would perceive Hufbauer's strategic tax policy as a "fair" method of taxation.

The examples of foreign tax systems leave many choices for policymakers. However, the taxation of foreign corporations is in fact much more complex than even the stylized examples noted above. The maze of complexities presently in any country's tax system means that a tax system will not easily be categorized as capital-export or capital-import neutral. Uncovering the role that taxation may play in the mobility of capital across countries requires substantial knowledge of tax systems. The brief overview provided below of the tax practices as they apply to major investors in the United States will lead to more precise formulations of empirical models of the tax systems and to more exact interpretations of our empirical results.

Tax Practices That Apply to Foreign Corporations

Most countries operate either a residence-based or a territorial tax system, although some countries use a combination of these two approaches.[14] The residence-based system is typical for most countries, including Japan, The United Kingdom and the United States. In countries operating a residence-based system, the foreign corporation is liable for host country taxes annually and for home country taxes when profits are repatriated to the parent corporation in the home country. Upon repatriation of net of foreign tax earnings to the home country, the home country statutory tax rate is applied to gross earnings (net earnings plus foreign taxes paid) and a tax credit is applied against the home country tax liability for taxes paid to the foreign country.[15] In practice, the tax credit is limited to the amount of home country tax liability. When the foreign tax liability is higher than the home country tax liability, the firm is in an excess credit position and essentially pays the foreign tax rate on its earnings.

For example, consider a U.S. corporation that locates a subsidiary in another country and retains the earnings within the subsidiary for some time. The foreign corporation would always pay taxes to the host country. In effect, if the corporation never repatriated the earnings to the United States, it would never pay U.S. taxes. However, if the corporation repatriates the earnings to the United States, the profits are then taxed at corporate rates in the United States. To avoid double taxation of the profits in the host and the home countries, the United States has established tax treaties with countries. The United States allows a tax credit for the foreign taxes paid up to the tax liability that would have been due in the United States.[16] Thus, if the host country taxes are higher than the home country taxes, the corporation pays no tax to the home country after applying the tax credit; the host country tax rates are effectively the tax rates for the corporation. If, on the other hand, the home country taxes are higher than the host country taxes, the corporation effectively pays the home country tax.

As explained above, the former situation amounts to a territorial tax system or capital-import neutrality. The latter case appears to be CEN (but see below), because capital that stayed within the United States and capital that moved overseas are both taxed at home country tax rates. Under CEN, it is worth reiterating, the incentive to invest overseas is governed by the rates of return to capital invested domestically compared to the rates of return to capital invested overseas. The tax system plays a neutral role.

Several countries, notably Belgium, France, the Netherlands, and Norway, operate a territorial tax system. Under that system, residents who invest in other countries are subject to the tax liabilities of the host country. The profits are never taxed in the home country.[17] A home country that operates a territorial tax system provides obvious incentives for residents to seek investment locations in host countries with lower tax rates.

To complicate matters, Canada and West Germany operate a mixed tax system for foreign investments.[18] Canada, for example, applies a residence-based tax system to foreign income with tax credits for foreign taxes paid. However, dividends earned in foreign corporations and repatriated to Canadian parent companies are not subject to Canadian (home) country taxes. Thus, for example, a Canadian subsidiary operating in the United States would pay home country taxes with a credit for taxes paid in the United States. However, Canada would not tax dividend income returned to the parent nor would it grant a tax credit for U.S. taxes paid on the dividend income.[19]

Beyond the aforementioned economic welfare implications of various tax policies, whether countries follow capital-export neutrality or capital-import neutrality determines whether home or host country tax rates are relevant for empirical work on the location decisions of foreign investment. To be more specific, United States federal and state corporate income tax rates can make a difference in the location choice of foreign investors in the United States only if U.S. (host country) taxes represent the marginal taxes on the investment. However, the following sections will argue that determining *a priori* whether foreign taxes are neutral in either an export or import sense is probably not possible.

Residence-Based Tax Systems, Deferral, and Capital-Import Neutrality

The literature on foreign taxation has until recently maintained that residence-based tax systems combined with a credit for taxes paid to foreign countries would produce capital-export neutrality. However, when tax deferral, or payment of home country taxes only upon repatriation of profits from foreign corporations, is layered onto the system, some argue that the tax system is no longer capital-export neutral (Caves 1982).[20] Hartman's (1985) analysis shows that residence-based tax systems with tax deferral until repatriation and tax credits for taxes paid to foreign governments are capital-import neutral rather than capital-export neutral. Hartman's analysis then implies that host country taxes could become a significant determinant of its inward foreign direct investment. (See appendix to this chapter for details on Hartman's argument.)

Additional Complexities

Since Hartman's paper, a number of authors have examined other aspects of the taxation of foreign direct investment.[21] The relatively straightforward tax systems presented so far have many additional complications. For example, host countries levy additional withholding taxes on dividends before they are repatriated to the home corporation. The withholding tax qualifies for the foreign tax credit in the home country. However, as the total amount of tax credit is limited to the total tax that would be due in the home country, the withholding tax can put the corporation into an excess credit position, meaning that it cannot use all of the tax credit.

The withholding tax and the possibility of excess credits may in turn alter corporate financial behavior. For example, instead of paying a dividend to the parent, the foreign corporation could pay interest on a loan from the parent. That strategy reduces the overall tax paid, as the interest payment is not subject to withholding tax and is also deductible from most corporate income tax bases in host countries. Thus, the interest tax payment is subject to only the home country tax rate.

There are several additional complications. Using transfer pricing, foreign corporations minimize aggregate tax burdens by transferring costs to the highest tax countries, or the corporations effectively realize profits or income in the lowest tax countries. There are also other limitations on credits for foreign taxes paid, such as the tax credit baskets defined in the 1986 U.S. Tax Reform Act. The baskets add further layers of intricacy to the system and help to make, a priori, the effect of taxes on foreign direct investment unpredictable. In such a complex system, empirical evidence can make an important contribution to our understanding of the role of taxation in FDI flows.

Given the different tax treatments on FDI among the four countries with the most investments in the United States, U.S. federal and state corporate income taxes are more likely to affect investment from the Netherlands and Canada with their territorial systems. There is more uncertainty about the importance of U.S. taxes on investors from Japan and the United Kingdom, which operate residence-based tax systems. Thus, in the empirical research presented later in this study, we distinguish between investors from countries with different treatments of taxes paid in the United States.

The Role of State Corporate Tax Systems

State tax systems introduce more layers of taxation on foreign source income and foreign investment. State corporate tax systems are by their nature complicated systems when corporations are active in more than one state. A host of complications are added to the system when corporations operate in more than one country.

To begin, corporate income taxes generally differ among states in the tax rates and the deductions and credits that determine taxable corporate income and tax liability. For example, corporations wholly resident within a state have their total corporate income after deductions subject to taxation. Corporations that operate affiliates in other states or in other countries can have a portion of their affiliates' income subject to taxation in the state. How much affiliated income is taxed in a state depends on the state's definition of an affiliate and on its formula to apportion corporate income to the state.

To explain more fully, general accounting practice would encourage corporations to report the corporate income separately for each of their affiliates, taking into account transfers among affiliates. Some states adopt separate accounting of corporate income for tax purposes, and corporations in these states are allowed to report taxable corporate income based on separate accounting of corporate income. However, because of the potential for corporations to avoid taxation in high-tax states through a system of transfer prices applied to commodity exchanges among affiliates, many states start with a broad definition of corporate affiliate income and then use a three-factor formula (the Massachusetts formula or its variants) to allocate a portion of the combined income to itself. Typically the amount of combined income allocated to a particular state is based on the share of combined payroll, sales, and property that resides in the state compared to the combined total payroll, sales, and property of the affiliates. The allocated income is then subject to the state's tax system.

States' definitions of an affiliated company differ substantially and, thus, corporate tax liabilities can depend heavily on the definition used to combine affiliates. For example, several states operate a unitary tax system in that they have a more spatially expansive definition of the corporation and its affiliates, resulting in higher corporate income attributable to the state.[22] The unitary states generally define a unitary business to include other corporate operations that contribute to the business conducted in the corporate group and that have 50 percent or more common ownership or control between the corporation located in the state and the corporate group. The group would then file a combined return for the state corporate income tax and use the three-factor allocation formula mentioned above (or a variant of it) to determine the proportion of the group income that is taxable in the state.

In fact, the unitary states operate one of two types of unitary tax systems—worldwide and domestic—with domestic being a less expansive definition of the corporation than worldwide. Under a worldwide unitary regime, any business located in the state would combine the income from worldwide affiliates fitting the definitions of a unitary business noted above. The worldwide definition includes in the apportionable tax base the foreign and domestic affiliates regardless of the place of incorporation, including the foreign parent and its foreign affiliates. Under a domestic unitary regime, the apportionable base includes both foreign and domestic affiliates of businesses incorporated in the United States, regardless of where they do business.[23]

During the period of our analysis, a considerable portion of states operated a worldwide unitary tax system. But the frequency of the worldwide unitary tax shrank from thirteen states in the early 1980s to five states by the end of our sample period or 1987. We account for this extreme form of unitary taxation in our empirical work.[24]

Other Taxes and Expenditures

International corporations and their employees face the same indirect taxes in host countries as do the domestic corporations in the host country. Thus, our full specification of the fiscal variables will account for sales, property, excise, and other taxes in our empirical models. Personal income taxes, while they are direct taxes, may also influence corporate location decisions to the extent that these taxes affect the type and number of employees in the labor supply. Personal income taxes will also be accounted for in the empirical work.

The expenditure side of state and local tax systems may also play a role in foreign corporations' choice of state. The sizable investments mean a substantial number of employees will consume schools, parks, highways, and other public goods. Higher taxes by themselves may not play a major role in location if the taxes purchase a desirable bundle of state and local goods and services. Thus, our empirical work will account for both the spending and revenue sides of state and local budgets.

Summary

We have examined the broader issues related to foreign investment. Our debtor nation status results from our negative portfolio investment position, although our surplus position in FDI continues to shrink. We highlighted the advantages of attracting foreign investment, as it adds to the productivity of our economy and in the shorter-run allows us to increase our consumption temporarily and stall repayment of our deficit.

Despite the size of the investment positions in foreign countries, researchers have raised questions about the long-term mobility of international capital. By examining patterns of domestic saving and investment, capital mobility among countries appears imperfect, suggesting that domestic saving will determine national economic growth. Using an alternative approach to the issue, Frankel finds that the equality of covered-interest rates across countries suggests perfect capital mobility among countries.

The tax policy discussion suggests a variety of approaches to the taxation of international capital, and enumerates the variety of methods that countries actually use. The complicated tax systems actually deployed suggest that there may be significant tax incentives affecting the location of foreign direct investment. Others might contend that the complications of the system, such as of transfer pricing and tax deferral, allow corporations to engage in significant tax avoidance; taxes, therefore, affect their financial practices but do not affect their location decisions on foreign investments. Exactly how tax policy affects the movement of international capital or whether we want to affect its movement with tax policy is not well understood. With all the complexities involved in taxation of foreign income and the opportunities available to firms to adjust their tax burdens by altering their financial policies, it seems unlikely that taxation would overtly play a significant role in FDI decisions.

We restrict our empirical inquiry to FDI location choices within the United States. The variation in state tax rates may have only second-order implications for FDI location among the states, given the complexities that apply at national government levels. Nonetheless, even if nontax factors govern inter-country FDI decisions, the effects of state and local fiscal policy may influence intra-country FDI locations among states.

Our Research: Direct Investment in New Plants

As is clear from above, foreign investment stems from many different sources and takes a number of different forms. For example, before making an investment, a foreign investor can choose from a wide array of alternative investments at home and abroad. If the investor recognizes a market opportunity in the United States, he or she considers how best to compete in that market. The options include exporting output to the United States, purchasing a portion or all of an existing company in the United States, engaging in a joint venture with a U.S. investor, expanding an existing production facility, or building a new plant.

In the rest of this book, we use data from the International Trade Administration (ITA) to analyze the location of new foreign plants between 1979 and 1987, the last year the data are available. The ITA data for foreign investments report the number of new plants, acquisitions and mergers, joint ventures, equity increases, and plant expansions. The agency gathers the data from newspaper and journal announcements and from reports from other federal agencies. Once compiled, no attempt is made to determine whether the investment actually occurred. While the ITA data may not be quite as reliable as the mandatory reports on United States investments that foreign firms file with the Bureau of Economic Analysis (BEA), the BEA data do not contain information on new plants. The ITA, however, reports that their information on foreign direct investments is consistent with the BEA data. Despite that claim, Glickman and Woodward (1989) express some reservations about the ITA data, but acknowledge that it is the only data on new plant investment in the United States.

Indeed, we share their reservations about the ITA data, because no verification is done on whether the reported investment announcements actually materialized. However, while acknowledging the shortcomings of the data, we believe they are generally accurate.

The International Trade Administration data reveal that most foreign direct investments take the form of either an acquisition or expansion of an existing plant. Equity increases and corporate buyouts of existing companies may create jobs through managerial efficiencies or revival of moribund plants, but those employment benefits are less noticeable to policymakers and the public. We choose to examine the location of new plants with the idea that the so called "greenfield investments" (new plants) might be the most interesting for policymakers.

From a discovery perspective, a greenfield investment, compared to an acquisition or a joint venture, allows the investor almost complete freedom to select a new plant site and to choose among sites within the

United States. Thus, examining new plant locations has the advantage of giving us the most insight into the location factors that attract foreign investors.

To focus the discussion in the next chapters, using data from International Trade Administration of the Department of Commerce, there were 4,326 direct non-real-estate investments in manufacturing during the 1978 to 1987 period. The largest share of the investments were acquisitions and mergers followed by new plants and then plant expansions (see table 1.3). There were 1,396 new foreign plant locations in the United States between 1978 and 1987, and 1,197 of the plants were in manufacturing.[25] We examine the data on the 1,197 manufacturing locations and attempt to explain the choice of investors among the 48 continental states.

The International Trade Administration data suggest that investors from Japan were responsible for 34 percent of the new foreign plants located in the United States between 1978 and 1987 (see table 1.4). Investors from Canada, Germany, and the United Kingdom accounted for an additional 40 percent of new foreign manufacturing plants in the United States between 1978 and 1987. Investors from France, Switzerland and the Netherlands accounted for another 14 percent of the new foreign manufacturing plants in the United States.

Also shown in table 1.4 is the distribution of the new plant investments by two-digit SIC code within the manufacturing sector. Of the 1,197 new manufacturing plants for the 1978 to 1987 period, 57 percent are concentrated in four industry groups; namely, Chemicals and Allied Products, Industrial Machinery and Equipment, Electronic and Other Electric Equipment and Transportation Equipment.[26] At the other extreme, there were no new plants in Tobacco Products, Apparel, and Other Textile Products; and Leather and Leather Products each had only five new foreign plants during the 10-year period. The balance of the new plants were distributed more evenly throughout the remaining 13 two-digit manufacturing industries (see figure 1.3).

The concentration of new manufacturing plants in four industry groups holds when new plant investments are examined by country. Canada investors have 46 percent of their number of new manufacturing plants in the same four industry groups noted above, and German investors have 67 percent of their new plants in those same four indus-

Table 1.3 Number of Non-Real-Estate Investments in Manufacturing Industries by Year and Type of Investment 1978 to 1987

Year	Acquisitions and mergers	Equity increase	Joint venture	New plant	Other	Plant expansion	Total
1978	107	19	13	56	53	7	255
1979	130	13	22	175	97	68	505
1980	187	26	29	171	34	79	526
1981	160	17	28	107	23	44	379
1982	107	21	41	81	34	40	324
1983	119	22	24	116	29	93	59
1984	161	25	47	190	43	92	558
1985	189	15	27	63	32	24	350
1986	222	25	28	95	40	41	451
1987	290	34	55	14	34	948	619
Total	1672	217	314	1197	434	492	4326

SOURCE: U.S. Department of Commerce, International Trade Administration (various issues).

NOTE: These data represent investments with complete information on the transaction site. There are some transactions for which no location information are available. The transactions are relatively few in number.

Table 1.4 Number of New Manufacturing Plants by Industry Group and Home Country of the Foreign Investor: 1978-1987

Two-Digit SIC Codes	Canada	France	Germany	Italy	Japan	Korea	Netherlands	Sweden	Switzerland	United Kingdom	Other	Total
20 Food and Kindred Products	6	4	4	3	21	2	4	0	7	3	10	64
22 Textile Mill Products	3	0	7	1	7	2	2	0	1	4	3	30
23 Apparel and Other Textile Products	0	1	0	0	1	0	1	1	0	0	1	5
24 Lumber and Wood Products	4	0	6	0	4	1	0	0	0	3	4	22
25 Furniture and Fixtures	3	0	1	0	1	0	1	0	2	1	3	12
26 Paper and Allied Products	9	0	3	0	3	0	0	3	0	3	2	23
27 Printing and Publishing	4	2	4	0	5	2	0	0	1	2	3	23
28 Chemicals and Allied Products	11	16	48	3	39	0	9	10	18	28	14	196
29 Petroleum and Coal Products	2	2	2	0	0	0	4	0	1	4	1	16
30 Rubber and Miscellaneous Plastics Products	4	2	1		1	15	0	6	1	2	8	10
31 Leather and Leather Products	0	0	1	2	1	0	0	0	0	0	15	
32 Stone, Clay, and Glass Products	2	5	13	2	12	0	0	0	4	5	9	52

Two-Digit SIC Codes	Canada	France	Germany	Italy	Japan	Korea	Netherlands	Sweden	Switzerland	United Kingdom	Other	Total
33 Primary Metal Industries	11	6	1	1	17	0	7	0	1	8	8	60
34 Fabricated metal Products	4	3	13	0	13	0	0	1	2	11	4	51
35 Industrial Machinery and Equipment	11	4	53	4	70	2	2	6	9	16	10	187
36 Electronic and Other Electric Equipment	17	5	21	2	92	6	3	5	5	10	9	175
37 Transportation Equipment	10	10	16	1	67	3	1	4	1	11	4	128
38 Instruments and Related Products	1	2	9	2	20	0	2	3	6	3	4	52
39 Miscellaneous Manufacturing Industries	3	4	2	2	14	0	1	1	1	3	5	36
Column Total	105	66	215	24	402	18	43	35	61	123	105	1,197

SOURCE: U.S. Department of Commerce, International Trade Administration, Foreign Direct Investment in the United States, various issues.

try groups. Japan and the United Kingdom have similarly large proportions of their new manufacturing plants in those four industry groups.

Foreign New Plants Compared Against America's Industrial Structure

The concentration of new foreign plants in four major industry groups might be expected if one could compare them to the major group concentrations of new plants built by domestic investors. With no access to data on new domestic manufacturing plants, we compared the industrial concentrations of new foreign manufacturing plants during the 1978 to 1987 period to the stock of assets in each major manufacturing group (see table 1.5) for all foreign firms and all businesses located in the United States in 1987. Four major groups, Chemicals and Allied Products, Petroleum and Coal, Food and Kindred Products, and Electric and Electronic Equipment, account for about 66 percent of total foreign assets in manufacturing. For all businesses, assets in six industries, Petroleum and Coal, Transportation Equipment, Chemicals and Allied Products, Food and Kindred Products, Machinery Except Electrical, and Electric and Electronic Equipment, account for 70 percent of assets in manufacturing. With the exceptions of Petroleum and Coal and Food and Kindred Products, new foreign plants are constructed in four of the major manufacturing groups that dominate the manufacturing assets held in the United States (see figure 1.4). Thus, based on asset data, we conclude that new foreign manufacturing plants are built in major industry groups where investments are already concentrated.

Outline of the Monograph

In chapter 2 of the book, we examine the patterns of new plant locations within the United States. We then examine the empirical evidence on the location of foreign direct investment among countries and what role taxes and other factors play in the foreign investors' decision. Next, we summarize the literature on the location choices that foreign investors make among states.

32

Figure 1.3 New Manufacturing Plants by Industry

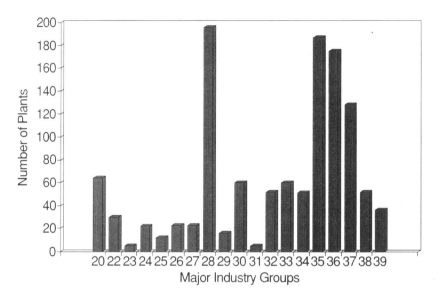

Figure 1.4 Assets of Manufacturing and New Foreign Plants, Six Major Industry Groups

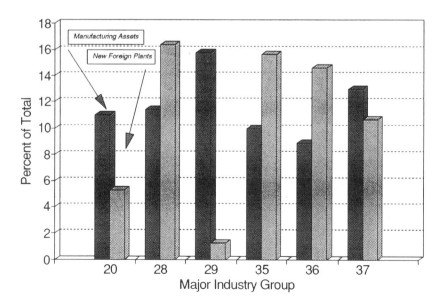

Table 1.5 Total Assets of U.S. Affiliates, All U.S. Businesses, and New
Manufacturing Plants, 1987

Industries	United States affiliates	All United States businesses	New plants
Stone, Clay and Glass	5.4	2.3	4.3
Chemicals and Allied Products	27.3	11.4	16.4
Primary Metals	5.4	3.7	5.0
Petroleum and Coal	21.1	15.8	1.3
Rubber and Plastics	2.1	2.1	5.0
Food and Kindred Products	10.0	11.0	5.3
Electric and Electronic Equipment	7.3	8.9	14.6
Printing and Publishing	3.8	4.7	1.9
Instruments and Related Products	2.8	3.7	4.3
Fabricated Metal Products	2.8	4.1	4.3
Paper and Allied Products	2.2	4.0	1.9
Machinery, Except Electrical	4.4	10.0	15.6
Textile Products	0.5	1.4	2.9
Transportation Equipment	2.7	13.0	10.7
Other	2.2	3.9	6.3
Manufacturing	100.0	100.0	100.0

SOURCES: Howenstine (1989); and U.S. Department of Commerce, International Trade
Administration (various issues).

In the third chapter, we discuss how to model the location decision.
There are numerous theoretical and econometric choices about modeling the location decision, and we discuss the background behind them.
We also lay out the econometric models that we use. In chapter 4, we
discuss the econometric estimation and present the results of the estimation. A fifth chapter contains some of the policy implications of this
research that flow from the simulation results reported there. Chapter 6
summarizes our findings and reports the conclusions from this
research.

Appendix to Chapter 1

To understand Hartman's (1985) analysis and conclusion that residence-based tax systems are capital-import neutral, it is helpful to distinguish between mature and immature foreign corporations. Mature foreign corporations fund their own reinvestment out of retained earnings, while immature corporations require transfers from the domestic parent to finance their investment. Hartman's conclusion applies to mature corporations only. His conclusions also require the full offset of foreign direct taxes against home country taxes. The implication is that home country tax rates are higher than host country tax rates.

Hartman first shows that mature corporations with unexploited investment opportunities in the host country would not simultaneously receive transfers from the parent to finance investments, while making dividend payments to the parent. This feature greatly simplifies the analysis, and the income of mature firms flows only in one direction. Hartman then examines the mature firm's decision either to return dividends to the parent for investment in the home country or to invest in the host country. If the firm returns a $1 dividend net of foreign taxes to the parent immediately, the dividends are incremented by the foreign taxes deemed paid on the dividends, or by $1/(1 - t^*)$, where t^* is the foreign tax rate and is assumed less than the home country tax rate of t. After paying the home country tax and accounting for the tax credit for foreign taxes already paid in the host country, the corporation pays a total tax rate of t—the domestic tax rate—on the gross earnings. Thus, the corporation has $[(1 - t)/(1 - t^*)]$ to invest at home. The net return to the repatriated profit at the end of the next period is $[(1 - t)/(1 - t^*)](1+r_n)$, where t is the domestic tax rate and r_n is the net rate of return to investment in the home country.

On the other hand, the firm can retain foreign earnings in the host country for one year and repatriate the profits after a second year. In this case, the net profit is $[(1 - t)/(1 - t^*)] [1 + r^*(1 - t^*)]$, where r^* indicates the rate of return on investment in the host country. Comparing the rates of return for home and host country investments, the firm will return dividends if the after-tax rate of return is higher in the home country (r_n) than the after-tax rate of return in the host country $[r^*(1 - t^*)]$. Thus, the net rate of return on investment and not the tax due upon repatriation affects the decision to reinvest.

The important conclusion from Hartman's analysis is that there is capital-import neutrality (not capital-export neutrality) as a result of the tax credit and deferment, because the firm's investment abroad is determined by the rate of return in the host country as is the domestic investment in the host country.[27]

NOTES

1. Unless otherwise noted, foreign investment refers to inward foreign investment or investment in the United States. In the few instances when we discuss investment flows from the United States to other countries, we use the term outward investment.

2. The period of analysis is dictated by data availability. The source of the data is the U.S. Department of Commerce, International Trade Administration. While similar data on individual plant locations are also available for the 1972 to 1977 period, it is our feeling, after examining the data quite thoroughly, that the data before 1978 have many more problems with missing values and other discrepancies than the post-1977 data.

3. For a discussion of the Department of Commerce's definition of foreign investment as distinguished from investment in plant and equipment, see Slemrod (1989).

4. Investment is defined as the flow of capital typically during a one-year period. Investment position is the stock of investment at a point in time.

5. Current-cost reflects the replacement cost of the capital stock after accounting for depreciation, depletion, and expensed exploration and development costs. Market value reflects valuation of capital stock based on valuation in the stock and bond markets. The valuation could be subject to short-term changes in valuation of stocks or bonds and year-to-year changes in market value may not reflect accurately investment flows. For more detail see Scholl, Mataloni, and Bezirganian (1992) and references therein.

6. Furthermore, the U.S. Department of Commerce data on foreign investment includes only four benchmark or complete survey years: 1959, 1974, 1980 and 1987. Foreign investment data for interim years are based on sample data from quarterly surveys and extrapolations from the benchmark survey years. The data thus calculated are never revised when new benchmark results are tabulated. (Slemrod 1989 and Glickman and Woodward 1989 (pp. 303-308) also note these limitations in the foreign investment data.)

7. We examine aggregate trends in foreign investment, using the U.S. Department of Commerce, Bureau of Economic Analysis data. The micro data in their raw form from the U.S. Department of Commerce, International Trade Administration, are not necessarily an accurate description of aggregate totals.

8. Feldstein and Bacchetta (1991) address the Obstfeld objection by adding economic growth and distribution variables to their savings-investment retention equation. They find that the growth argument does not diminish the strength of the relationship between domestic saving and investment. Williamson (1991), however, casts doubt on the relationship, arguing that domestic saving and investment are not strongly correlated. Therefore, the marginal flows of international capital could play a critical role in a country's capital accumulation leading to more economic productivity. A separate issue is the effect of saving and investment on productivity growth in an economy. Baumol, Blackman, and Wolff (1989) accept the view that productivity growth leads to saving and investment rather than saving and investment fostering productivity.

9. Covered-interest parity means that capital flows would equalize interest rates across countries when similar investments in the two countries are contracted in the same currency. For example, suppose a dollar-based investor contracted a three-month dollar denominated deposit and a three-month German mark denominated deposit together with a three-month forward contract to change German marks into dollars. As both investments are contracted in a common currency and the yields are known in advance, covered-interest parity simply means that the two investments yield the same return. This example is taken from *The Economist* (1992).

10. Note that CEN could also be achieved under a territorial tax system if all host countries allowed investment expensing.

11.The deduction of foreign taxes paid from income before calculating home country taxes due leads to gross returns to domestic country investment equal to net of tax returns for foreign country investment. For example, a home country domestic investor would receive after-tax income of $r_d - t_d\, r_d$, where r_d is the gross return to a dollar of domestic investment and t_d is the domestic tax rate. With deductibility for foreign taxes paid, a foreign investor would receive after-domestic-and-foreign-tax income of $r_f - t_d\,(r_f - t_f\, r_f) - t_f\, r_f$, where r_f is the gross return to foreign investment and t_f is the tax rate in the foreign country.

Investors would maximize capital income when they equate the after-tax rates of return in both countries or when $(1 - t_d)\, r_d = (1 - t_d)\, r_f - (1 - t_d)\, t_f\, r_f$ or $r_d = r_f - t_f\, r_f$. The latter condition implies that the tax deduction for foreign taxes leads investors to equate the gross return on domestic investment to the net of tax return on foreign investment. For more discussion of taxation of foreign capital as well as its welfare implications, see Allworth (1988).

12.Hufbauer (1992) suggests maintaining residence-based taxation for foreign portfolio investment, as returns to capital more likely influence portfolio capital flows among countries.

13.Reich (1990) makes a similar case about firm location among countries and argues that industrial policy in the United States might be used to attract high-tech firms.

14.This discussion of residential and territorial tax systems is based in part on Slemrod (1989).

15.The United States tax code does not extend depreciation and investment tax credits to foreign firms when profits are repatriated to the United States. Thus, foreign corporations, held by U.S. investors, pay the statutory corporate income tax rate (see Gordon and Jun 1992).

16.The United States has operated a foreign tax credit system since 1921. The foreign tax credit can take two forms: a credit for the total taxes paid to foreign governments or a credit given for each country in which the corporation has an investment. There may be certain investment advantages to a per country credit system if a corporation is in an excess credit position overall but not in a country in which it intends to invest more capital. From 1921 to 1932 the credit was a worldwide or overall limitation. Between 1932 and 1954, foreign tax credits were limited to the lesser of the overall limitation or a limitation of credit per country. From 1954 to 1960, a per country tax credit limitation was in effect; from 1960 to 1975 the corporation was allowed to choose between a per country and the overall limitation. Since 1975 the overall limitation has been in effect (see Joint Committee on Taxation 1987, Title XII, p.855).

17.Capital-export neutrality is violated under a territorial tax system unless the home and host country tax systems happen to be the same.

18.For more discussion of foreign taxation in other countries, see Hines and Hubbard (1989).

19.The Canadian exemption of repatriated dividends from home country taxation stems from the exemption of all intercorporate dividends from further taxation. The exemption avoids the double taxation of dividends, as they have already been taxed as profits before distribution as dividends (see Kitchen 1987, pp. 357-358).

20.In fact, Horst (1977) states erroneously that the tax rate on foreign investment is a weighted average of the home and host country tax rates, as repatriated profits are taxed at home country rates and retained earnings are taxed at (relatively low?) host country rates. Thus, the residence-based U.S. tax code was alleged to favor foreign investment over domestic investment and that pushed the U.S. Congress to introduce a number of tax bills in the 1960s and 1970s that would have eliminated the deferral of home country taxes on retained earnings of foreign corporations (Horst 1977). The repeal of tax deferral never passed Congress, however.

21.For a discussion of other aspects of the taxation of foreign direct investment in the United States, see Hines (1988), Jun (1989), Goodspeed and Frisch (1989), Hines and Hubbard (1989), Altshuler and Fulghieri (1990), Sinn (1990), and Hines and Rice (1990). Hufbauer (1992) provides a blueprint for reforming U.S. taxation of foreign income.

22.Some states, although not unitary *per se*, enforce strict rules about combining business income for affiliates and corporations that have joint stock ownership and other aspects in common, although the affiliates do not operate in their state. In effect the state operates a form of unitary taxation without being called a unitary state.

23.Some states operate a domestic waters edge combination which combines incomes only of affiliates doing business in the United States. For a discussion of the unitary tax see Moore, Steece, and Swenson (1987) and Hellerstein (1983). The discussion above relies extensively on information provided in both of these sources. For a discussion of affiliated business groups, see New York State Department of Taxation and Finance (1992).

24.We did not account for domestic unitary taxation in our analysis, although several other authors have found its coefficient statistically significant in their analysis of the locations of foreign plants. We believe that their findings may be a statistical artifact, as many of the domestic unitary states, such as Idaho, Montana, Nebraska, and Utah, are very small and would probably have few foreign manufacturing plants locating there with or without a domestic unitary tax.

25.Manufacturing plants are those classified in SIC codes 20 to 39.

26.The so-called high-tech industries are categorized within these major industry groups. For a discussion of high-tech categories and the merits of high-tech firms, see Tyson (1992).

27.Hartman departs from Horst's (1977) analysis pointing out that Horst ignored the future home country liabilities for foreign investments. Thus, averaging the host and home country tax rates was not correct. Hartman points out that Horst's average tax rate results result from his failing to take account of taxes ultimately due on repatriated foreign investment. Horst in effect treats deferral as an exemption from home country taxes on retained earnings or as if retained earnings will never be repatriated.

2
Location Choices
of
New Foreign Plants
in the
United States

Building on the empirical trends in chapter 1, we begin here by examining the location patterns of new foreign manufacturing plants in the International Trade Administration data base from 1978 to 1987. Plant location is examined by country of origin for the four leading investors as well as for the total of all foreign plants. We identify some distinct concentrations of new foreign plants in particular states.

We next examine the findings and methodologies of empirical studies of foreign direct investment. There are two types of studies in the empirical literature. The first focuses on the determinants of aggregate flows of FDI among countries. This literature will help us decipher how important such variables as national tax policy and aggregate location determinants are to FDI flows among countries. Unfortunately, the empirical literature does not test exactly the many aspects of the theories of aggregate FDI flows examined in chapter 1, but we are able to draw some implications from the findings.

A second strand of the literature examines the determinants of FDI location among states within a given country or among a set of countries located in a particular region, such as the European Economic Community (EEC). We gain additional insight into why FDI might locate in particular states of the United States and whether the policy levers available to state governments can make a particular state more attractive to foreign plants and investors. Finally, we compare the location results obtained for foreign investors to the results obtained in the firm location literature in general. Are foreign investors looking for something different in their locations from what domestic investors are looking for?

Location of New Foreign Manufacturing Plants in the United States

As noted earlier, foreign investors located 1,197 new manufacturing plants in the United States between 1978 and 1987. Figure 2.1 maps the concentration of the 1,197 new plants by state. The largest concentrations of new manufacturing plants occur in seven states: California, Texas, Tennessee, Georgia, North Carolina, Illinois and New York. Together, these states account for 47 percent of the total number of plant locations during the 1978 to 1987 period. Those concentrations aside, foreign investors locate the vast majority of their new manufacturing plants in the eastern half of the United States.

Seventy-four percent of the new foreign manufacturing plants are from four countries: Canada, Germany, Japan, and the United Kingdom. The next four figures illustrate the concentrations of new plant locations in states by country of the major investor. The 105 Canadian plant locations are heavily concentrated in New York State, which has 26 percent of the new Canadian plants (see figure 2.2). North Carolina accounts for another 10 percent of the new Canadian plant locations. Tennessee and California each had about 8 percent of the new Canadian plants.

German plant locations are displayed in figure 2.3. Connecticut, New York, Virginia, North Carolina, South Carolina, Georgia, and California account for 45 percent of the 215 German plant locations in the United States during the 1978 to 1987 period. The 215 plants are also heavily concentrated in the eastern states.

By contrast, new Japanese plant locations are heavily concentrated in California, Washington, and Texas (see figure 2.4). These three states account for 30 percent of the 402 new Japanese plants locating in the United States during the 1978 to 1987 period. Another six eastern states—Ohio, Georgia, North Carolina, Tennessee, New Jersey, and New York—account for 33 percent of Japanese new plants. United Kingdom investors concentrate 54 percent of their 123 manufacturing plant locations in eight states, namely, North Carolina, Texas, Georgia, Florida, New Jersey, Tennessee, Connecticut, and Ohio (see figure 2.5).

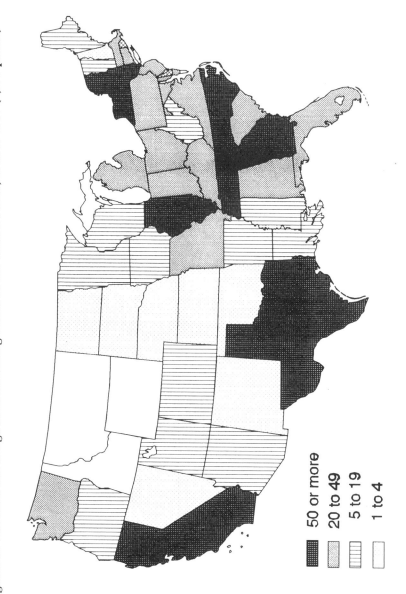

Figure 2.1 Location of Foreign Manufacturing Plants in the United States, 1978 to 1987 (1,197 plants)

50 or more
20 to 49
5 to 19
1 to 4

42

Figure 2.2 Location of Canadian Manufacturing Plants in the United States, 1978 to 1987 (105 plants)

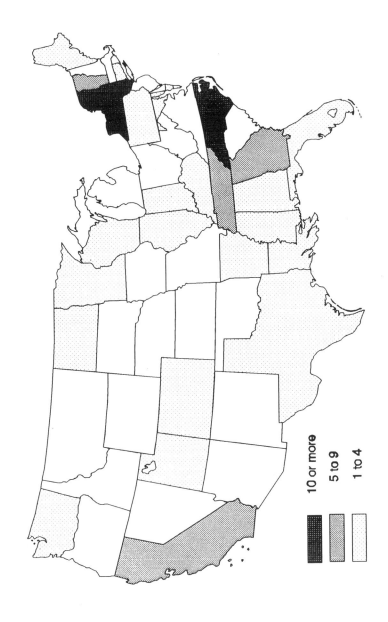

10 or more

5 to 9

1 to 4

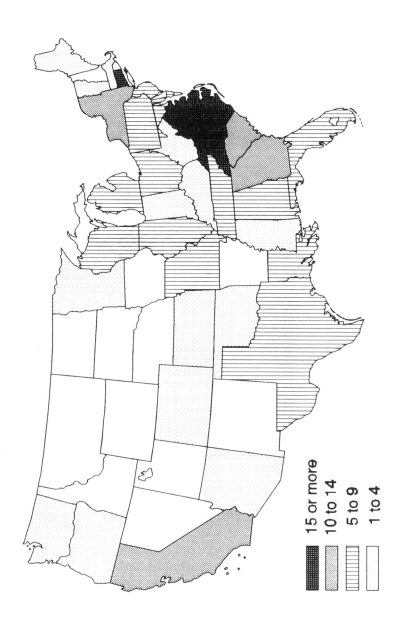

Figure 2.3 Location of German Manufacturing Plants in the United States, 1978 to 1987 (215 plants)

15 or more

10 to 14

5 to 9

1 to 4

44

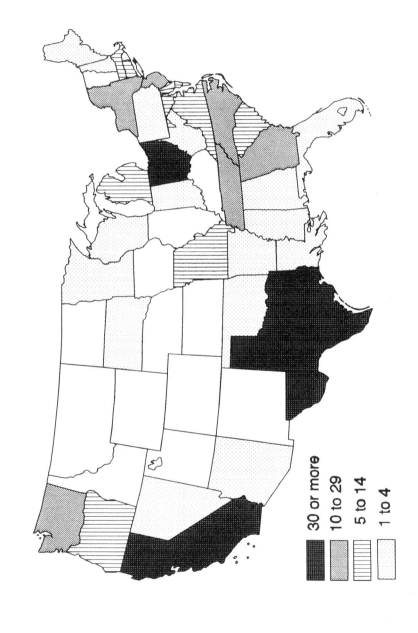

Figure 2.4 Location of Japanese Manufacturing Plants in the United States, 1978 to 1987 (402 plants)

30 or more
10 to 29
5 to 14
1 to 4

Several interesting patterns appear to emerge. For example, these foreign investors tend to locate their plants in states that are geographical nearer their own country. The Canadians have heavily concentrated their locations in New York State, while Germany and the United Kingdom have concentrated their investments in the Eastern states. Japanese investors appear to prefer states on the West Coast. North Carolina, and to some extent Georgia, are also popular location choices for all four countries, while Tennessee was a popular location for three of the four countries.

Concentration of Industry in States

As noted in chapter 1, about 57 percent of the 1,197 new foreign manufacturing plant locations during the 1978 to 1987 period are in four major industry groups: Chemicals and Allied Products (196 plants), Industrial Machinery and Equipment (187), Electronic and Other Electric Equipment (175), and Transportation Equipment (128). Plants in these major groups cluster in from five to nine states, depending on the major industry group. For example, 47.5 percent of the plants in the Chemicals and Allied Products category are concentrated in five states: Texas, followed by North Carolina, New Jersey, Georgia and Delaware (see table 2.1). About 60 percent of the foreign plants in the industrial machinery and equipment group are concentrated in nine states, with the largest concentrations in North Carolina, California, Connecticut and Georgia, and lower concentrations in Tennessee, Texas, New York, Illinois, and Michigan. Overall, about 61 percent of the foreign plants in Electronic and Other Electrical Equipment are concentrated in eight states, with California and Georgia having 28 percent of the foreign plants. Plants in this major group also concentrate in North Carolina, Texas, Tennessee, New York, Indiana and Delaware. Almost 69 percent of the foreign plants in transportation equipment are concentrated in the auto alley states and California, New York, and Texas. For example, over 15 percent of the new plant locations are in Ohio, while foreign plants in the Transportation Equipment group are also concentrated in Michigan, Tennessee, Kentucky, Illinois, and Indiana.

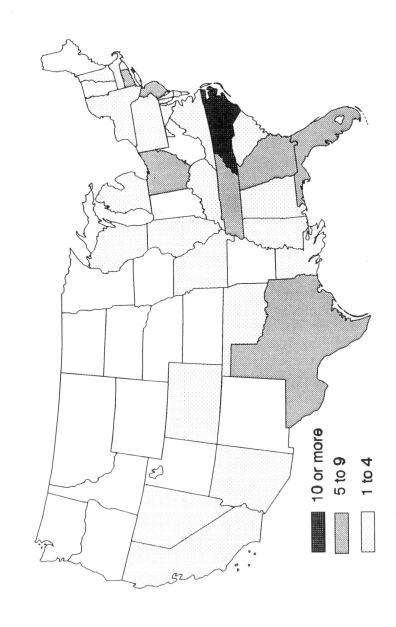

Figure 2.5 Location of United Kingdom Manufacturing Plants in the United States, 1978 to 1987 (123 plants)

Table 2.1 State Concentrations of New Foreign Plants for Four Major Groups (percent of new plants by major industry group)

	Chemicals and Allied Products (28)	Industrial Machinery and Equipment (35)	Electronic and Other Electrical Equipment (36)	Transportation Equipment (37)
Alabama	6.1			
California		8.0	17.2	7.8
Connecticut		8.0		
Delaware	4.1			
Florida			4.6	
Georgia	4.1	7.0	10.9	
Illinois		5.4		6.2
Indiana			.6	5.5
Kentucky				7.0
Michigan		4.3		8.6
New Jersey	8.2			
New York		5.9	5.1	4.7
North Caro-lina	8.7	9.1	6.9	
Ohio				15.6
Tennessee		5.9	5.1	7.8
Texas	16.3	5.9	6.9	5.5

SOURCE: U.S. Department of Commerce, ITA data on new plants.
NOTE: If more than 4 percent of the new plants in a major group are located in a state, it qualifies here as a concentration of the industry.

We cannot explain here the strong concentrations of new plants in particular states. The location patterns may be tied to industry agglomeration economies available in each state or to the availability of a known workforce or environment due to previous investments in the states. In the latter case, the locations may not appear to represent the most attractive locations when a standard set of cost and market variables is examined. However, when considerations internal to the firm enter the calculations, the observed locations dominate the alternatives.

For example, if a number of Canadian subsidiaries are already located in New York State, the firm may consider locating an additional plant there rather than in another state, even though the latter state now appears to have lower costs. The firm can probably spread internal economies of scope, such as managerial expertise, more easily among plants located in proximity to one another than when plants are located in areas more remote from one another.

In addition, there is some evidence (Tyson 1992) that Japanese firms locate plants producing automobiles as well as parts suppliers in close proximity to one another to increase parts and product reliability and the overall quality of the final product. That practice, if followed, would also help to account for high concentrations of firms from a particular country in particular states. It seems unlikely that empirical work could account for many of these variables. Nonetheless, we will attempt to account for the concentrations of firms in particular locations, even if we cannot totally explain the reasons for the concentrations. Put another way, we also recognize that concentration economies internal to the firm and other than the industry agglomeration economies that are measured with published data might explain the observed concentrations of these industries.

Aggregate Foreign Direct Investment Studies

The recent literature on aggregate FDI flows among countries follows two distinct courses. One strand focuses almost exclusively on U.S. corporate tax policy as a determinant of the volume of FDI in the United States. A second strand largely ignores corporate tax policy and focuses on nontax economic determinants of FDI. The main features and findings of eight major studies that focus on determination of FDI flows among nations are summarized in table 2.2.

Do Taxes Matter in Aggregate Investment Decisions?

Hartman (1984) has pioneered the recent empirical work on FDI in the United States, or at least the work that emphasizes the effect of taxes on FDI flows. His research, while omitting many other determinants of foreign investment, relates inward U.S. FDI to rates of return on investment variables and to the relative U.S. tax rates faced by foreign and domestic investors. Following his distinction between mature and immature investors (mentioned in chapter 1), Hartman examines separately investments of existing foreign subsidiaries financed by retained earnings (mature firms) and investments financed by transfers of funds from parent corporations. In both cases, however, Hartman finds that the relative effective U.S. tax rates faced by foreign and domestic investors significantly affect FDI within the United States. In all of the regressions that he runs with aggregate data from the 1965 to 1979 period, the elasticities of inward investment flows to the United States with respect to the relative tax rates are significantly larger than unity, and in some cases the elasticity estimates are larger than two. His results reveal a substantial role for corporate tax policy in attracting and maintaining FDI flows into the United States. However, the regressions explaining FDI financed by transfers from parent corporations fit the data less well than the regressions for FDI financed by retained earnings. The former elasticities are also less statistically significant compared to the latter case. Nonetheless, while he appropriately cautions about the simplicity of the model specification, Hartman finds that U.S. tax policy significantly affects inward FDI. Hartman's empirical results are also consistent with his theoretical analysis, which led him to suggest that there is capital-import, but not capital-export, neutrality.

Hartman's pathbreaking work in this area set the tone for this line of research. For example, subsequent papers follow his separate analyses of investment financed from transfers and from retained earnings. The research also shares his emphasis on the role of tax policy.

Boskin and Gale (1987) update Hartman's analysis using revised measures of effective tax rates and conduct the analysis over different time periods. Their results for the 1965 to 1979 period are similar to Hartman's, although Boskin and Gale's point estimates of the parameters, while still elastic, are somewhat smaller than Hartman's. When they also analyze U.S. inward FDI during the 1956 to 1984 and the 1965 to 1984 time periods, they find that FDI was more responsive to tax differentials after 1965, and elasticities of investment with respect to the various specifications of the tax rates for the 1965 to 1984 period are similar to the estimates that Hartman finds.

Table 2.2 Results From Studies of the Determinants of FDI Flows Among Countries

Study	Country of analysis and period	Principal findings
Hartman (1984)	FDI inflows to U.S. from 1965 to 1979. FDI financed from retained earnings and transfers from parent corporations analyzed separately. Variables are relative return on investments and U.S. tax rates faced by foreign and domestic firms.	Taxes have a substantial effect on inward FDI flows. Elasticities of FDI with respect to taxes range from above unity to just above two, and are generally larger for FDI financed from retained earnings than from transfers from parents. Equations explaining FDI from transfers fit less well than those explaining FDI from retained earnings.
Boskin and Gale (1987)	FDI flows to U.S. from 1956 to 1984. They adapt Hartman's model by using an updated series on effective tax rates and adding a GNP variable and a dummy variable for the 1980s.	For 1965 to 1979 period, results are similar to Hartman's. Augmenting the model with GNP and other variables does not alter the basic results. The elasticities of FDI with respect to taxes are higher in the 1965 to 1984 period than in the 1956 to 1984 period. Retained earnings fit the equations better than transfers from parents.
Young (1988)	Inward FDI to U.S. from retained earnings and transfers using revised data on effective rates of return. Data are for 1956 to 1984. Basic Hartman models are augmented with a lagged dependent variable and a GNP variable.	In the augmented model, elasticities of retained earnings with respect to tax rates and rates of return are smaller than Hartman and Boskin and Gale find. Young finds that FDI financed from transfers from parents are inelastic with respect to both taxes and rate of return variables.
Slemrod (1989)	FDI flows into the U.S. by country of investor: Canada, France, Netherlands, West Germany, Italy, Japan, United Kingdom. The first four countries operate territorial tax systems and the last three operate residential tax systems. Also explains total FDI, FDI financed from retained earnings and from transfers from parents. Time period is from 1960 to 1987 or 1962 to 1987 (for two countries).	Variables include GDP in home country relative to GDP in U.S., unemployment rate of prime-age males in U.S., real exchange rate of U.S. dollars relative to the home country's real exchange rate, and the Auerbach and Hines (1988) measure of the marginal effective corporate income tax rate on fixed investment in the U.S. Coefficients for real GDP and real exchange rates generally have the correct signs and are statistically significant. The coefficients on the tax variables reveal no strong role for taxes in either territorial or residential tax countries.

Cushman (1987)	U.S. FDI inflows and outflows to and from five countries: Canada, Japan, United Kingdom, France, Germany. Data from 1963 to 1981.	FDI inflows to the U.S. increase with its real GNP, a lower dollar exchange rate, and a stable exchange rate. However, higher wages in the U.S. and higher productivity in the home country reduce the FDI inflow to the U.S.
Culem (1988)	FDI inflows among six industrialized countries (U.S., Germany, France, United Kingdom, Netherlands, Belgium), 1969-1982. Analyzes FDI inflows into all six countries, inflows from U.S. to EEC countries, inflows from EEC to U.S., and inflows among EEC countries only.	The pooled results for all countries in the sample indicate that higher real GDP in the host country, a wider gap between real GDP in the host and home countries, and higher home country exports to the host country increase the FDI flow to the host country. Higher labor costs in the host country reduce FDI inflows, however.

FDI flows from the EEC countries to the U.S. increase with a higher GDP in the U.S., higher tariff rates in the U.S., and higher exports from the home country to the U.S. |
| Ray (1989) | FDI flow into U.S. by industry from these countries: Japan, Canada, total of EEC countries. 1979 to 1985. | The principal findings suggest that U.S. GNP growth increases FDI inflow from other countries to the U.S. Except for Japan, where the exchange rate has no effect on FDI flow, a low-dollar exchange rate increases FDI inflow to the U.S. Higher growth in a four-digit industry within the U.S. leads to more FDI in that same industry. |
| Mann (1989) | Japanese FDI in U.S. for 12 major manufacturing groups 1977 to 1987. Examines Japanese investment in new plants, increases in Japanese equity holdings in existing manufacturing firms in U.S., and total investment in new plants and equity increases. | Higher savings in Japan, higher U.S. nontariff barriers, and higher sales of the product by firms already in the U.S. increase equity, new plant, and the total of equity and new plant investments. Higher raw material costs in the U.S. reduce equity investment and total investment, but not specifically new plant investment. Higher world interest rates reduce new plant investment and total investment, but not investment to increase equity.

Dollar-yen exchange rate and labor costs in the U.S. have no effect on equity and new plant investments in the U.S. |

They then depart from Hartman's empirical specification and augment the right-hand-side tax variables with a GNP variable and a time dummy variable equal to unity for the 1980s and zero otherwise. However, the new variables do not affect the elasticities for the tax variables. Also consistent with Hartman, Boskin and Gale find that the regressions examining investment financed by retained earnings fit the data much better than the regressions examining investment financed by transferred capital.

Young (1988) further modifies the Hartman model by introducing a lagged dependent variable and a GNP variable on the right-hand-side. Young finds FDI financed from retained earnings less responsive to both the tax and the rates of return variables than both Hartman and Boskin and Gale. Furthermore, the responsiveness of transferred funds to both the tax and rates of return variables is less than unity or inelastic. Young's results indicate a diminished role for taxation in U.S. inward FDI financed from transferred funds. His results also imply that the simple Hartman model might not be the most appropriate for examining FDI flows, especially FDI flows financed by funds transferred from foreign parent corporations.[1]

Slemrod (1989) also tests the influence of taxation on FDI in the United States during the 1956 to 1984 period. He augments Hartman's model with additional macroeconomic variables and also tests the proposition that U.S. taxes have more influence on investors from countries operating a territorial tax system than investors from countries operating a residential tax system with a credit for foreign taxes paid. He finds evidence that U.S. taxes affect total FDI and net transfers from abroad, but do not affect FDI financed from retained earnings. He also finds that whether a country operates a territorial or residential tax system has little influence on FDI flows.

The recent studies examined here in the end find a limited role for tax policy in the explanation of the aggregate flow of direct investment into the United States. For example, when more variables are added to the original models, the conclusion that taxes have a strong effect on FDI collapses. In addition, the econometrics used to estimate the models in the later papers is more sophisticated or the estimators are more efficient and likely to be more accurate. Measures of the tax variables themselves have also become more sophisticated; earlier tax variable measures might be erroneous.

But should not tax factors make a difference? Why should we accept the findings of no tax effects if our intuition suggests otherwise? Recall that Gordon and Jun, as well as our argument in chapter 1 describe the complexity of the taxation of foreign capital flows. The possibilities to avoid capital taxation through timing of repatriations and adjusting financial behavior could lead to a neutral effect of taxation on aggregate financial flows. However, underneath the aggregate data may be substantial tax effects on financial transactions that are designed solely to reduce the tax impact on capital income. Thus, while aggregate studies may fail to identify tax effects, the effects may indeed be substantial. We suggest that taxation can affect aggregate capital flows even if and because corporate financial policy is designed to neutralize the effects of taxation on capital flows.

Other Influences on FDI Flows

Several researchers perform time-series or pooled cross-section/ time series analyses that all but ignore taxation issues and focus on other economic dimensions of the foreign investment decision. Several of the studies examine FDI inflows into the United States as well as into other major countries, while others confine their inquiry to U.S. inflows of FDI. Four of these studies are summarized in the latter half of table 2.2. There is some consensus among the research findings, although the findings do not always point in the same direction. In some cases, for example, the conflicting evidence garnered from studies of combined FDI flows from several countries into the United States is reconciled when the flows are examined by country of origin.

Wage Effects

Earlier empirical literature found no evidence (Dunning 1980) that higher wages influenced FDI.[2] Among the four studies (Cushman 1987; Culem 1988; Ray 1989; and Mann 1989) summarized in table 2.2, Cushman, examining U.S. FDI inflows from and outflows to the five other major investing countries during the 1963 to 1981 period, finds that host country wages are a statistically significant determinant of FDI inflows to countries. A related finding is that higher productivity in the home country of the investor leads to less FDI outflow to other countries. Similarly, Culem finds that host country unit labor costs deter FDI inflows into particular European Economic Community (EEC) countries. To be specific, unit labor costs did not affect the aggregate size of the FDI flowing to the EEC, but unit labor costs determine to some degree the location choice for the FDI or the destination of FDI within the EEC countries. The latter is an important observation for our research on FDI location within the United States, because relative wage costs among the states may attract (or deter) FDI to (from) certain states. More to the point, Culem finds that wage costs do not influence the aggregate flow of FDI to the United States; he did not test, however, the location choice of FDI among states.

Market Variables: Gross Domestic Product, Tariffs

Five of six major studies (Cushman 1987; Ohullachain 1984; Mann 1989; Culem 1988; and Ray 1989) find that the level of Gross Domestic Product (GDP) and the growth of GDP in the host country attract FDI especially in the case of the United States (Caves 1982 is the sixth study). According to these studies, one attraction of FDI is access to the American market place. The studies are divided about the importance of tariffs and other trade barriers. Caves, Culem and Mann find that the circumvention of trade barriers is an important incentive to invest directly in the trade-restricting country, while Ray and Cushman find no evidence that tariff barriers influence FDI flows.

Exchange Rates

The literature is less divided on the role of exchange rates and exchange rate stability. While not all studies examine the role of exchange rates in FDI flows, studies that include exchange rates in the analyses conclude that devaluation of the host country currency relative to the home country currency accelerates FDI, except in the case of Japanese investors. Studies examining only Japanese FDI in other countries find no role for exchange rates.

Levinsohn (1989) points out, however, that a role for exchange rates in FDI is unexpected. If the U.S. dollar, for example, is low relative to its equilibrium value, firms could earn profits by arbitrage in the foreign exchange market for dollars without accelerating FDI. Nonetheless, in many cases lower-priced dollars accelerate FDI even if the exchange rate does not influence the location or type and size of the investment.[3]

Lessons for States

What can state policymakers learn from this literature on aggregate investment flows? First, if wages are important to the investor, they are more likely to influence the firm's location within the United States rather than affect the decision about the aggregate size of FDI in the United States. To be specific, the choice to enter the United States is mainly determined by the size of the market for the product and by growth in that market. More populous states or ones near large concentrations of population may fare better in attracting foreign investors.

United States tariff and nontariff barriers are important influences on the volume of FDI into the United States. Industries that face significant U.S. trade barriers are particularly good candidates for recruitment to a state. In addition, recruiting foreign investment may be easier when the U.S. dollar is weak relative to other currencies.

According to Ray, FDI in the United States tends to be in those industries that are also growing domestically in the United States. The evidence shown in figure 1.4 and table 1.5 of chapter 1 tends to support the conclusions of Ray's study. Thus, states should not necessarily look for foreign investors who will replace the dying industries in their states with those same industries. In all likelihood, the FDI will be in the very industries that prosper domestically. Thus, states that have a workforce trained in a dying industry will still want to think about retraining programs to make their workforce suitable to growing industries within the United States, as opposed to attracting foreign investors who will utilize the existing skills of the displaced workers. Another implication growing out of Ray's findings is that states will want to be careful in offering generous tax and other concessions to attract foreign investors, especially when the concessions could give an advantage to foreign firms relative to domestic firms in the same growing industries within the state.[4]

Studies of FDI Location Within the United States

Table 2.3 summarizes seven major studies performed on FDI location within the United States during the 1980s. With the exception of the Glickman and Woodward (1987) research, all of the studies use

Table 2.3 Summary of Selected Studies of FDI Location in the United States from 1980 to 1989

Study	Data/time period/sample	Estimation method	Variables with statistically significant coefficients and their effect (+ or -) on FDI
McConnell (1980)	1976 cross-section of 2,151 acquisitions, mergers or new plants.	Dependent variable: share of the total investment in each state. Ordinary Least Squares stepwise regression applied to a list of right-hand-side variables.	• Agglomeration economies (+) • Urbanization (+) • Population Density (+) • State located in the manufacturing belt (+) • State and local expenditures per capita (+) • Index of social well-being (-) • Distance from New York City (-) • Federal aid to state and local governments in the state (-) • Manufacturing employees per capita (-) • Retail sales per capita (-)
Shetty and Luger (1985)	Pools ITA data, for years 1979, 1981, 1982, 1983. Total of 76 new plant start-ups in three industry groups: SIC 38 (drug manufacturing) SIC (355,356 (industrial machinery) SIC 371 (motor vehicle production).	Conditional multinomial logit for locations among states of new plants in each industry group	• Agglomeration economies (+) • Wages (-) in two of three regressions • State policy index (+) in two of three regressions
Moore, Steece and Swenson (1987)	Net foreign investment in manufacturing assets by state for 1977 to 1981.	Dependent Variable: net foreign investment in gross assets by state. Regressions for each year from 1977 to 1981	• Business Climate (+) • Population (+) • Unemployment (+) • Worldwide unitary (-) • Domestic unitary (-)
Glickman and Woodward (1987)	BEA series on U.S. affiliate employment; employment growth between 1974 and 1983 in foreign manufacturing plants in each state.	Ordinary Least Squares	• Gravity measure of market in state (+) • Percent change in per capita income (+) • Right to work law (-) • State spending per capita (-) • Montana and Wyoming dummy variable (+) • Ratio of farm population to manufacturing employment (+) • Worldwide Unitary Taxation (-)

Study	Data	Methodology	Variables
Friedman, Gerlowski, Silberman (1989)	Number of new manufacturing plants in states for the 1976 to 1986 period.	Ordinary Least Squares performed on total, high-tech and nonhigh-tech manufacturing plants. Independent variables averaged over the 1976 to 1986 period.	• Market potential (gravity measure) (+) • Wage (-) (in total and high-tech manufacturing only) • Scientists and Engineers per capita (+) (in high-tech manufacturing only) • State has a container port (+) • State dollars spent attracting FDI (+) (for total and non-high-tech manufacturing)
Coughlin, Terza, Arromdee (1991)	ITA: Number of FDI investments in each state in 1981, 1982 and 1983. (Investments include new plants, acquisitions, mergers, joint ventures, and other investments.)	Conditional logit model.	• State land area (+) • Income per capita (+) • Production worker average wage rate (-) • State unemployment rate (+) • Manufacturing employment per square mile (+) • Unitary taxation (-) in two of four equations • Infrastructure variables (highways, RR miles, and airport facilities per square mile) (+)
Woodward (1992)	Japanese-affiliated manufacturing investments, 1980-1989. Data from Japan Economic Institute. Total sample of 540 plants.	Two levels of analysis: Selection of states, selection of county within state. Uses multinomial logit analysis; independent variables are for 1980. For the county-level analysis, the estimation is performed separately on a sample of total counties, auto-alley counties and non-auto-alley counties.	State Choice: • Gravity measure of per capita income of state location (+) • Unionization rate (-) • Domestic unitary tax (-) • Worldwide unitary tax (-) • State office in Japan (+) • Land area of the state (+) • Pacific region of U.S. (+) • East North Central region of U.S. (+) • East South Central region of U.S. (+) County Choice: • Manufacturing agglomeration (+) • Population density (+) (Total and non-auto-alley only) • Interstate highway connection (+) • Poverty rate (-) (total and non-auto-alley only) • Nonpoor black density (-) (auto-alley only) • Unemployment rate (-) (total and auto-alley) • land area (+)

micro data to analyze location choice. However, the studies vary in their level of econometric sophistication and disaggregation of the analysis. For example, in some cases the sample sizes are very small (Luger and Shetty 1985), making their results potentially unreliable. Two of the studies, McConnell (1980) and Coughlin, Terza, and Arromdee (1991), are performed on a single year of data for the explanatory variables, while the other studies examine growth or start-ups over a multiple-year period. Two studies (Luger and Shetty 1985 and Friedman, Gerlowski, and Silberman 1989) distinguish new plants from other investments, but others perform the estimation on the entire group of new investments mixing acquisitions and joint ventures, for example, with new plants.

Despite considerable methodological differences among these existing studies, they share several findings. Agglomeration economies, urbanization economies, and measures of market demand are important in attracting FDI to states. On the other hand, higher wages and worldwide unitary taxation deterred FDI within the states. Higher taxation in general, right-to-work laws, and unionization of the workforce, however, are generally not found to have a statistically significant effect on FDI in states.

While as a group the above studies reach similar conclusions, it is premature to regard the results as conclusive. Analysis using other data sets and further disaggregation of the data might generate different results for particular industries or home countries. Woodward's 1992 study examines the location of Japanese manufacturing firms within the United States and is an example of how disaggregation of the data and the location decision can produce refinements in the conclusions.

It is worth describing his analysis and results in more detail here. He uses micro data for the 1980 to 1989 period on 540 plant locations obtained from the Japan Economic Institute and performs two levels of analysis: state choice and the selection of the county within the state. For the state analysis, he finds that higher per capita income in the region, a state economic development office located in Japan, the state's land area, and the state's location in the Pacific region, in the East North region, or in the East South region attracts Japanese manufacturing plants. On the other hand, a high level of unionization of the labor force in the state and unitary taxation deter Japanese manufacturing locations.

For the county-level analysis, he first examines counties in a pooled analysis and then disaggregates the counties into auto- and non-auto-alley counties within the United States.[5] The auto-alley countries are those lying in the states between Michigan and Tennessee. Manufacturing agglomeration economies, an interstate highway connection, and counties with larger land areas attract more plants in the pooled and in each of the auto- and the non-auto-alley county analyses. A higher population density in a county attracts more plants in the pooled county-level analysis and in the non-auto-alley analysis, whereas higher rates of poverty and unemployment deter Japanese manufacturing plant locations in these same two types of counties. Property taxes do not influence plant locations in any of the county-level analyses.

Another finding is noteworthy. A higher percentage of blacks in the population deters location of Japanese manufacturing plants in the auto-alley counties. Woodward's finding on spatial discrimination is somewhat surprising, although racial discrimination by the Japanese has been the subject of some speculation.

Cole and Deskins (1988), for example, argue that Japanese auto producers, and possibly other foreign investors, located in the United States effectively discriminate against blacks. By selecting rural sites for their plants, they employ fewer blacks than is typical in the industry. Furthermore, Cole and Deskins point out that states offering subsidies to foreign investors who practice discrimination against certain minorities by locating in certain rural counties may, in effect, be subsidizing discrimination against blacks and other minority populations. While this is an interesting finding that needs further testing, a state-level location analysis such as ours is not likely to uncover such discrimination patterns.   Thus, while our results provide insight into the location decision at the state level, states should be aware of the potential for more subtle patterns of location within their state and the potential for discrimination.

Comparing the FDI Location Results with the General Location Literature

Numerous location studies of domestic firms and employment exist. Bartik (1991) cites 57 interarea studies or those that examine locations decisions among states or among metropolitan areas. As Wasylenko's

(1991) review also suggests, the results of these studies vary considerably. Most of the studies have focused on manufacturing employment, and that aspect of the work is consistent with the focus of the FDI studies.

Below we review the major results for the existing studies and point out consistencies with the results for FDI locations. While certain patterns emerge, we emphasize that the results are not uniform across studies, subjecting interpretations of the results to considerable judgement.

Wages

Wages represent a major component of costs and higher wages are expected to deter growth in manufacturing. A more productive labor force will lead to higher wages, so that wages must be compared to productivity measures. The latter variable is generally not observable, and many researchers develop proxy measures for productivity, such as the median number of school years completed by the adult population of an area. The productivity proxy measures are at best imperfect, and the studies do not adequately correct the measured wages levels for productivity differentials. Differences in productivity across areas and across time may account for the variation in results for the wage variable among studies.

The majority of location studies find that areas with higher wages attract fewer manufacturing jobs over time, but in many cases the coefficients on the wage variables are not statistically significant. The FDI studies reviewed here have nonuniform results for wages, suggesting in about half the cases that differentially higher area wages reduce the chances of attracting a new foreign manufacturing plant or investment. The nonrobust results for the wage variable are surprising, given the significance of wages in the costs of manufacturing. However, when the coefficients on wages are not statistically significant, other unmeasured factors, such as productivity or other endowments in the regions, may help to explain the attractiveness of the regions to some manufacturers, despite higher wages levels.

Unions

Unions can affect labor costs in several ways. Unions can raise wage and fringe benefits levels. The former effect should be captured in the wage variables, but to the extent that unions raise fringe benefit levels, unionization will have an impact on labor costs not already reflected in the wage level.

In addition, unionization can create a climate of tension between labor and management that reduces worker productivity. In some cases, union effects on productivity are more explicit. For example, union leaders have at times introduced work rules, such as assignment of a specific number of workers to a production process, leading to lower output per worker. A strike can produce an untimely disruption in the workplace.

The percentage of the U.S. manufacturing labor force that is unionized declined from 27.3 percent in 1984 to 23.8 percent in 1991 (U.S. Bureau of the Census 1992). The decline in unionization has largely tracked reduced employment in high-wage manufacturing jobs. Efforts to unionize nonmanufacturing sectors of the economy have not offset the losses in the manufacturing sector. Global competitiveness has also induced some unions to become more cooperative with management in some labor disputes, because both parties have realized that competition threatens corporate profitability and jobs at the corporation.

Unions can also improve the labor environment for management. For example, Freeman and Medoff (1984) suggest that a unionized firm can have higher productivity due to higher capital-labor ratios, less worker turnover, and the attraction of higher quality labor to unionized firms. Lower worker turnover, for example, reduces training costs and raises plant-specific human capital, which could account for the observed higher productivity.

The mixed *a priori* effects of unionization are reflected in mixed results for the unionization variable in business location studies. Many location studies find that unionization *per se* has no effect on business location or employment growth. Nonetheless, the issue is not settled, because other researchers find that unionization affects employment growth in manufacturing industries in general and in foreign manufacturing locations in particular. However, given the reduced coverage and influence of unions, their impact on location outcomes, while unsettled, is probably declining in significance.

Agglomeration Economies

There is strong and consistent evidence that specific types of firms are attracted to similar places. Agglomeration may bestow benefits, for example, from vertical interactions between firms that sell intermediate inputs and firms that purchase the inputs. The agglomeration of firms may also result in the attraction of a greater number of skilled workers to reside near the firms, and the skilled workers may in turn attract more firms. Thus, measures of agglomeration economies persistently turn up significant positive coefficients for manufacturing location decisions in both the general and the foreign manufacturing location literature.

Fiscal Variables

Fiscal variables have generated more controversy than any of the other findings. In part, policymakers have direct control over expenditures and tax levels and that heightens their interest in the effects of fiscal variables on job creation. Studies vary significantly in the sophistication with which they handle fiscal variables. Few studies use the balanced-budget technique of Helms (1985), which includes all expenditures and taxes in the estimated equation. Most studies include a portion of the tax and expenditure variables or leave out the expenditure side completely. Thus, the comparability of the results across studies is especially difficult in this case.

In the general literature on business location and employment growth, tax variables and public expenditure variables are statistically significant in a number of studies. Bartik (1991) has assessed this literature and concludes that in the majority of studies, tax variables influence business location of manufacturing firms. Wasylenko and McGuire (1985) contributes to the evidence on significant tax effects.

Many of the studies that find significant effects for fiscal variables in manufacturing are performed on data from the 1970s. Wasylenko has attempted unsuccessfully to reproduce the tax results using data from the 1980s. Carroll and Wasylenko (1993) examine specifically whether the data for the 1970s follow a different regime than data for the 1980s. Indeed, the regimes are different and manufacturing employment growth responds to fiscal variables for the 1970 data but not for the 1980 data. It appears that fiscal differentials narrowed among states in the 1980s, making the fiscal differentials less significant as a location or growth determinant.

Those findings cause us to examine the existing literature on fiscal effects in a different light. Many of the studies that use 1980 data, including the studies of FDI reported here, do not find statistically significant effects for the fiscal variables. Thus, the general level of taxation in a state does not appear to affect FDI. However, none of the studies includes expenditure variables in the analysis.

Foreign firms are concerned with more than the general level of taxation in a state, however. As noted in chapter 1, a state's use of worldwide unitary or domestic unitary taxation affects the taxable status of the firm's profits in other countries. Most of the FDI empirical studies examine worldwide unitary taxation and find that states using that form of taxation to determine taxable profits have a lower probability of attracting foreign investors. The two studies that include domestic unitary taxation in the model find that its use also dampens FDI activity in the state.

Closer inspection of the states that use domestic unitary taxation makes us cautious about accepting the conclusion about its dampening effects. Moore, Steece, and Swenson (1987) list Colorado, Illinois, Kansas, Massachusetts, Montana, Nebraska, and Utah (and in practice New York) as domestic unitary states. But three of the domestic unitary states (Montana, Nebraska, and Utah) have virtually no new foreign plants located in them (see figure 2.1) and three others (Colorado, Kansas, and Massachusetts) have a small number of foreign plants in them. The domestic unitary tax variable may pick up regional effects or isolate states that have few if any foreign firms for reasons unrelated to the domestic unitary tax. Put more directly, the results on the domestic unitary tax variable may be spurious.

In summary, we believe that there are broad similarities between the existing studies on general firm location and the studies on FDI. However, the latter area is still not thoroughly explored, and further studies may identify wider gaps between the location decisions of foreign and domestic firms.

NOTES

1. In addition, Newlon (1987), as summarized in Shah and Slemrod (1990), replicates the Hartman and Boskin and Gale models and identifies mistakes in the calculations of rate of return in the data set used in their analysis. When he applies the corrected data to the 1965 to 1979 period, he finds that the retained earnings equations do not fit as well as when they are fitted with the unrevised data, but the transfer equations fit somewhat better using the revised data as compared to the fits using the unrevised data. However, when Newlon analyzes FDI from 1956 to 1984, none of the coefficients in the transfer equation is statistically significant.

2. For a review of the earlier literature, see Caves (1982).

3. While the review of the literature has focused on FDI into the United States, the Shah and Slemrod (1990) study of FDI in Mexico deserves mention due to its thoroughness and interesting findings. Shah and Slemrod examine FDI in Mexico during the 1965 to 1987 period. Their model accounts for host and home country taxation and incorporates Mexico's tariff policy, credit worthiness, and an index of the regulatory environment. In addition, they incorporate Mexico's marginal effective tax rates into their analysis, arguing that marginal tax rates are better indicators of the incentives to invest. They also include average effective tax rates for the U.S. in their model. For the transfers equation, the coefficients on the marginal effective tax rate in Mexico and credit worthiness are statistically significant and indicate that higher tax rates and worse credit ratings reduce FDI transfers from abroad. For the retained earnings equation, the coefficients on credit worthiness, marginal effective tax rates in Mexico and average tax rates in the home country are statistically significant and affect FDI in the hypothesized ways. Thus, Hartman's hypothesis about the insignificance of home country tax rates is not confirmed. Moreover, Mexico's tariff structure and its regulatory environment do not influence its inward FDI.

4. A reviewer has pointed out that Ray's finding that FDI industries are similar to industries growing in the United States may not be particularly robust over time. The reviewer cites the automotive sector as a counterexample to the Ray conclusion. The reviewer may be correct for that particular industry. We note, however, that Ray's measure of domestic industry growth is the increase in the value of product shipped and not employment growth. The implication is that manufacturing industries with large productivity gains may experience relatively large gains in the value of shipments but slow employment growth or even employment losses. If employment is used to gauge industry growth patterns, the domestic growth industries could appear to be declining rather than growing.

5. To keep the data-gathering manageable, Woodward's sample includes all counties that have a Japanese manufacturing plant located in them and a random sample of nine counties in each state that do not have a Japanese manufacturing plant located in them.

3
Modeling the Location
of New Plants

In principle at least, the choice of a state for the location of a new plant seems straightforward. The firm would examine the potential profits to be earned in each state and choose the state that offers the highest profit.

In practice, the location choice is much more difficult for a host of reasons. Firms will presumably have a long-range definition of profits in mind, and in that case the firm will choose states that have favorable economic variables now and favorable expected economic variables over the profit horizon of the plant. Firms might use the information on all past values of the relevant economic variables in an attempt to make forecasts about their future values. However, unless we know exactly how this is done, there seems to be little hope that we would be able to duplicate such a method independently. We therefore assume in our analysis that the current values of the relevant variables are the firms' best forecasts for future values.

Furthermore, it seems unlikely that we, as researchers, will be able to identify or use all the relevant variables that go into the firm's decision. Accordingly, we will subsume all of the relevant variables that we cannot identify or use into a random component that acts like a disturbance in a linear regression model.

The subjection of profits to a random component allows us to use econometric methods to identify the influence of each identified independent variable on the probability of location in a particular state. However, the choice of an econometric method to use on the problem is fraught with several ponderous estimation issues.

In this chapter, we first address the conceptual profit maximization problem and discuss the general class of econometric estimation models that are consistent with the profit maximization problem. After that, we point out the limitations of the most straightforward econometric model within the class and then turn to refinements of the basic estimation model that will lead to more reliable estimates of the model's coefficients.

Maximizing Location Choice and a Baseline Estimation Method

We follow the typical modeling approach to location choice. The firm selects a state site for a new plant by examining a vector of its potential profits across the 48 states, π. The firm chooses the state corresponding to the element in π with the highest profit level. If we let π_i denote the firm's forecasted profits in state i, then state i is chosen only if

$$\pi_i = \max (\pi_1, \ldots, \pi_{48}) . \tag{3.1}$$

We, of course, only observe the firm's choice of state for location of the plant, and do not observe the firm's forecasts of its profits at each site.

While we do not observe the forecasted profits, we can infer the important determinants of these profits by analyzing econometrically the choices that firms actually have made. We postulate *a priori* that they are a function of observed characteristics in each state, such as wages, agglomeration economies, fiscal variables, and other variables which we will discuss in the next chapter. Write these observed characteristics as a vector X_s for state s.

Forecasted potential profits in each state s can now be written as a function of X_s and a random error, ε_s,

$$\pi_s = X_s \beta + \varepsilon_s , \tag{3.2}$$

where β is the vector of estimated coefficients. Therefore, a particular state i is chosen if

$$X_i \beta + \varepsilon_i > X_s \beta + \varepsilon_s \quad \text{for} \quad s \neq i. \tag{3.3}$$

The standard assumption is that the residuals ε_s are independently and identically distributed as a type I extreme-value distribution (also called a Weibull distribution), which has a cumulative distribution function of

$$F(\varepsilon) = \exp\left(-\exp(-\varepsilon)\right) . \tag{3.4}$$

Then the probability of choosing a given state i can be expressed as

$$P(i) = \exp\left(X_i\beta\right) / \sum_{s=1}^{48} \exp(X_s\beta) \tag{3.5}$$

The baseline estimation is a standard multinomial logit estimation. Many computer software packages will readily produce estimates of the β coefficients. However, the standard multinomial logit estimation method involves a very strong assumption that the addition of a state to the choice set or the deletion of a state from the choice set does not affect the relative probabilities of the choice of state i and state j. This property, known as the "independence of irrelevant alternatives" (IIA), means that the relative probabilities of choosing a location in New York and in Pennsylvania, for example, are not affected when North Carolina or Texas are removed from the choice set of locations. Put differently, if, for example, North Carolina is removed from the choice set of locations, the probabilities of choosing New York and of choosing Pennsylvania are changed in the same direction and by an equal percentage.

The presence of the IIA property can be demonstrated using equation (3.5). The relative probabilities of choosing any two states depend only on the information in X for the two states in question. In our New York (NY) and Pennsylvania (PA) example,

$$P(NY) / P(PA) = \exp(X_{NY}\beta) / \exp(X_{PA}\beta) . \tag{3.6}$$

In moving from (3.5) to (3.6), the denominator on the right-hand-side of equation (3.5) cancels out of the numerator and denominator of (3.6). With the elimination of the denominators, the information in the vector X for North Carolina is removed or becomes irrelevant to the relative probabilities of locating in New York or Pennsylvania.[1]

From an economic or analytical perspective, the imposition of the IIA property means that the relative probability over two location choices does not depend on the existence of close substitutes for either location. To many analysts such an assumption seems overly restrictive and unrealistic. Nonetheless, research in this area has applied the standard multinomial logit model to location choices. We examine some alternative estimation methods below.

Nested Multinomial Logit

For the choice of location among 48 states, the nested multinomial logit model (NMNL) developed in McFadden (1978) postulates residuals that have a generalized extreme-value distribution; the distribution avoids the IIA assumption.[2] McFadden also showed that the NMNL model can be derived from a stochastic utility or in our case a stochastic profit-maximization model.

The NMNL model takes advantage of a hierarchical decisionmaking structure. In our problem, for example, we can assume that firms make location decisions sequentially. They choose a region of the country and then choose a state within the chosen region. The NMNL model carries two advantages. The standard multinomial logit model is nested within it and thus when we estimate the simple NMNL model, we can detect, based on the value of a parameter, whether the IIA assumption is appropriate.

To present this advantage in more detail, we present succinctly the mathematics of the simple NMNL model and relate the analysis presented above to the relevant parameters of the model.

The Simple NMNL Model

The firm will choose a region r and then a state i within the region. The choice of region and state will then be the probability of choosing state i given the region r multiplied by the probability of choosing the region r. In symbols,

$$P(i, r) = P(i|r) \cdot P(r) . \tag{3.7}$$

The conditional and marginal probability can be rewritten as

$$P(i|r) = \exp(X_i\beta) / \sum_{s\varepsilon r} \exp(X_s\beta) \tag{3.8}$$

and

$$P(r) = \exp(Y_r\alpha) \sum_{s\varepsilon r} \exp(X_s\beta) / \sum_{r'} \exp(Y_{r'}\alpha) \sum_{s'\varepsilon r'} \exp(X_{s'}\beta) , \tag{3.9}$$

where the outer summation in the denominator of (3.9) is taken over all regions r'. Here Y_r is the vector of attributes that vary only with region r.

Now define an inclusive value I_r as follows:

$$I_r = \log \sum_{s\varepsilon r} \exp(X_s\beta) .$$

This allows us to rewrite equations (3.8) and (3.9) as:

$$P(i|r) = \exp(X_i\beta / \exp(I_r) \tag{3.10}$$

and

$$P(r) = \exp(Y_r\alpha + I_r) / \sum_{r'} \exp(Y_{r'} \alpha + I_{r'}) . \tag{3.11}$$

So far, equations (3.10) and (3.11) simply amount to estimating the standard multinomial logit model, because the joint choice of region and state has been broken into a conditional probability framework (3.7). In a simple NMNL model, a single coefficient on the inclusive values can take on a value other than unity; this same factor also scales the deterministic component of each stochastic profit function. Thus, the simple NMNL model can be written as:

$$P(i|r) = \exp(X_i\beta / (1 - \sigma)) / \exp(I_r) \tag{3.12}$$

and

$$P(r) = \exp(Y_r\alpha + (1 - \sigma)I_r) / \sum_{r'} \exp(Y_{r'} \alpha + (1 - \sigma)I_{r'}) , \tag{3.13}$$

where the inclusive value is redefined as follows to reflect the scaling of the deterministic profit components:

$$I_r = \log \sum_{s \in r} \exp(X_s \beta / (1 - \sigma)) .$$

When $\sigma = 0$ or $(1 - \sigma) = 1$, the simple NMNL model becomes the standard multinomial logit model. When σ limits to 1 or $(1 - \sigma)$ limits to 0, it can be seen from equation (3.13) that the state-specific variables imbedded in I_r and $I_{r'}$ play no role in the selection of region r. In that case, the simple NMNL model implies that the choice of region and the choice of state within the region are completely separate.

The estimation of the coefficient of the inclusive value will reveal whether the IIA property and therefore the standard multinomial logit model is appropriate. A coefficient of unity for $(1 - \sigma)$ suggests that alternative choices are irrelevant for determining the relative probabilities between any two choices. However, if $(1 - \sigma)$ equals zero, state-specific characteristics introduce no interregional dissimilarities at the choice of region. Therefore, in the econometric literature, the coefficient $(1 - \sigma)$ is referred to frequently as the dissimilarity index or dissimilarity parameter.

McFadden showed that the simple NMNL model is consistent with stochastic utility or profit maximization as long as σ is between zero and unity (see also Daly and Zachary 1978). If the estimated coefficient value for $(1 - \sigma)$ falls outside of the unit interval or is not between zero and unity, the estimated coefficients of the model are not consistent with the profit maximization framework and the estimation model may be misspecified.[3]

The errors are assumed to follow a generalized extreme-value distribution function that allows the Weibull errors to be correlated among states within a region but not among states across regions. Maximizing the likelihood function based on the generalized extreme-value distribution function and estimating the parameters simultaneously and not sequentially produces full-information. Maximum likelihood estimates for α, β and $(1 - \sigma)$ are consistent, asymptotically normally distributed and asymptotically efficient (see Hensher 1986).

The third and final estimation model will relax the assumption that dissimilarity parameters are constant across regions and permit them to vary.

The Generalized NMNL Model

The final model that we will examine in this section is a nested multinomial logit model that allows each region r to have its own dissimilarity parameter $(1 - \sigma_r)$. To simplify the mathematical presentation, we will follow Börsch-Supan and define

$$\theta_r = 1 - \sigma_r .$$

The joint cumulative distribution function of the ε_{sr}'s for this new model is given by

$$F(\varepsilon) = \exp \left[- \sum_r \left[\sum_{s\varepsilon r} \exp \{- \varepsilon_{sr}\}^{1/\theta r} \right]^{\theta r} \right], \tag{3.14}$$

where ε is the vector of all stochastic components of profits across states. The function F is a member of the generalized extreme-value class of cumulative distribution functions, and when all θ_r's equal one, it describes the standard multinomial logit model.

From Theorem 1 of McFadden (1978), the cumulative distribution function in (3.14) with the following new definition of the inclusive value:

$$I_r = \log \sum_{s\varepsilon r} \exp(X_s\beta / \theta_r)$$

yields the following expression for the probability of choosing a particular region r

$$P(r) = \exp\{ Y_r\alpha + \theta_r I_r \} / \sum_{r'} \exp \{Y_{r'} \alpha + \theta_{r'}I_{r'}\} \tag{3.15}$$

in the generalized nested multinomial logit model. The conditional probability of choosing a particular state i given that its region r has been chosen is

$$P(i|r) = \exp(X_i\beta / \theta_r) / \exp (I_r) . \tag{3.16}$$

McFadden showed that, in an analogous manner to the simple NMNL, each of the dissimilarity parameters θ_r in the generalized nested multinomial logit model must be greater than zero and less than or equal to one, if the model is to be consistent with stochastic profit or maximization.[4]

To simultaneously estimate α, β, and the dissimilarity parameters, we maximize the likelihood function to obtain FIML estimates of the parameters which are again consistent, asymptotically normally distributed, and asymptotically efficient.

We will obtain estimates using all three of the logit models outlined above. The results are reported in chapter 4 after a description of the data and an outline of the hypotheses to be tested.

NOTES

1. The IIA property is often referred to as the red bus-blue bus problem, because the development of the standard multinomial logit model is rooted in a choice of transportation mode (McFadden 1974). In that context, the IIA property means that the probability of taking a red bus relative to the probability of taking a private automobile is independent of whether there also exists a close substitute for the red bus, such as a blue bus.

2. The multinomial probit model (MNP) does not impose the IIA assumption, and Hausman and Wise (1978) have applied the MNP model to a transit-choice problem. However, when more than four choices are involved, such as in our choice from among 48 states, the MNP model becomes impractical to apply. See Maddala (1986, p. 62) for a discussion.

3. Börsch-Supan (1990) argues that the condition that the dissimilarity parameter lies in the unit interval may be too strong. He shows that economic theory can rule out some values for profits or utility and then the dissimilarity parameter can be somewhat larger than unity without the coefficient estimates being inconsistent with the stochastic utility or profit maximization framework.

4. Börsch-Supan's (1990) criticism about the apparent restrictiveness of the theoretical boundaries on the dissimilarity parameter in a simple NMNL model can also be applied to the generalized NMNL model case.

4
Empirical Results and Analysis

In this chapter we present the results from our estimation of the statistical models discussed in chapter 3. We attempted several specifications for each of the three logistic models—the standard multinomial logit and the simple and generalized nested multinomial logit models—on a comprehensive data set containing information on the 1,197 new manufacturing plants built by foreign investing firms in the contiguous United States between 1978 and 1987. The data are described in detail, along with the hypotheses that we are interested in testing in our statistical analysis.

The estimation results for our preferred model—a standard multinomial logit specification with the State of California removed from the Mountain-Pacific region and becoming its own region—are presented together with the corresponding specification in which California is included in the Mountain-Pacific region. We also present a synopsis of results, including those for the simple and generalized nested multinomial logit models that led to our preferred specification and an analysis of the predictive ability of that specification. (A more detailed discussion of the results for the nested multinomial logit models is presented in appendix B to this chapter.)

Data and Hypotheses

In this section we outline the foreign investment data used in the statistical analysis, present the construction of the covariates or explanatory variables used in the logits, and describe the expected signs of the associated coefficients. The starting point for the foreign investment data was the information on the 1,197 new manufacturing plants built by foreign investing firms in the contiguous United States from 1978 to 1987, as recorded by the International Trade Administration (ITA) of the U.S. Department of Commerce. Besides information on the country of origin, the host state, and the year of the investment, the ITA provides information on the two-digit SIC classification code for the new plant and the investing firm's estimate of the value of the new plant.

We deleted a few observations from our analysis. For example, the home countries of the firms are from four continents: Europe, Asia, North America, and South America. To maintain a parsimonious analysis of the continent where the foreign investment originated, we deleted the observation on the single new plant built by a South American firm; we also deleted a new plant built by a Mexican firm, so that in our sample Canadian investors represent the only North American home country from which new manufacturing plants in the United States originate. Thus, the countries of origin, besides Canada, could be classified as coming from two regions, Europe and Asia, with 1,195 new plants left in the analysis at this point.

In addition, of these 1,195 new plants, 640 investing firms provided information on the investment value of the plant. Because we wanted to use plant value as one of the explanatory variables, we decided to attempt predictions for the missing values. As will be described below, we were able to provide predictions for 544 of the 555 missing cases. This means that 1,184 new plants were available for use in the logit analysis.

In the next subsection we describe the state-specific variables, as well as the expected signs for their associated coefficients. We then describe the region-specific variables in the following section. An exact description of all variables used in the analysis is given in table 4.1.

State-Specific Variables

We use wage rate, energy cost, population and fiscal information, as well as information on agglomeration economies and the proximity of the country of origin to the prospective host state to model the location choice among states. The right-hand-side variables are measured in each state at the time that the new plant is recorded in the ITA data set, and thus, the values of the covariates change over time.

In preliminary analysis, we included per capita income and growth in per capita income variables, following the lead of other researchers. The coefficients for the market variables generally had the wrong signs

Table 4.1 Variable Definitions

	Description
Continuous variables	
General state variables	
Real Wage	Real average hourly production earnings deflated with the GNP deflator. Varies with state and year. Logarithmically transformed in specifications. Source: U.S. Department of Labor, Bureau of Labor Statistics, State and Area Employment, Hours and Earnings, computer tape.
Employment Agglomeration	Two-digit SIC industry employment in state divided by total private employment in state. Varies with state, year and two-digit SIC code of investing firm. Source: U.S. Department of Commerce, Bureau of Economic Analysis, Table SA25, floppy disk.
Population	State Population (in millions). Varies with state and year. Logarithmically transformed in specifications. Source: U.S. Department of Commerce, Bureau of Economic Analysis, Table SA5, floppy disk.
Real Electric Bill	Average electric bills (in dollars) for the industrial sector (300 KW - 60,000 KWH) in state, deflated with the GNP deflator. Varies with state and year. Logarithmically transformed in specifications. Source: U.S. Department of Energy, Energy Information Administration, Federal Power Commission, Typical Electric Bills, selected years.
Real Gas Bill	Average price per 1000 cubic feet of natural gas (in dollars) for the industrial sector in state, deflated with the GNP deflator. Varies with state and year. Logarithmically transformed in specifications. Source: U.S. Department of Energy, Energy Information Administration, Natural Gas Annual, selected years.
State fiscal variables	
Intergovernmental Aid	State and local aid from the federal government, multiplied by 100 , then divided by state personal income (obtained from U.S. Department of Commerce, Bureau of Economic Analysis, Table SA5, floppy disk). Varies with state and year. Source: U.S. Department of Commerce, Bureau of the Census, Governmental Finances, selected years.
Deficit	State and local deficit defined as direct general expenditures minus total general revenues, multiplied by 100, then divided by state personal income (see above). Varies with state and year. Source: U.S. Department of Commerce, Bureau of the Census, Governmental Finances, selected years.

Continuous variables	Description
Health Expenditures	State and local health expenditures, multiplied by 100, then divided by state personal income (see above). Varies with state and year. Source: U.S. Department of Commerce, Bureau of the Census, Governmental Finances, selected years.
Highway Expenditures	State and local highway expenditures, multiplied by 100, then divided by state personal income (see above). Varies with state and year. Source: U.S. Department of Commerce, Bureau of the Census, Governmental Finances, selected years.
Primary and Secondary Education Expenditures	State and local expenditures for local schools, multiplied by 100, then divided by state personal income (see above). Varies with state and year. Source: U.S. Department of Commerce, Bureau of the Census, Governmental Finances, selected years.
Higher Education Expenditures	State and local higher education expenditures, multiplied by 100, then divided by state personal income (see above). Varies with state and year. Source: U.S. Department of Commerce, Bureau of the Census, Governmental Finances, selected years.
Other Expenditures	Other state and local expenditures, multiplied by 100, then divided by state personal income (see above). Varies with state and year. Other state and local expenditures computed as direct general expenditures minus health, highway, primary and secondary education, and higher education expenditures. Source: U.S. Department of Commerce, Bureau of the Census, Governmental Finances, selected years.
Property Tax	State and local property tax revenues, multiplied by 100, then divided by state personal income (see above). Varies with state and year. Source: U.S. Department of Commerce, Bureau of the Census, Governmental Finances, selected years.
Sales Tax	State and local sales tax revenues, multiplied by 100, then divided by state personal income (see above). Varies with state and year. Source: U.S. Department of Commerce, Bureau of the Census, Governmental Finances, selected years.

Continuous variables	Description
Individual Income Tax	State individual income tax revenues, multiplied by 100, then divided by state personal income (see above). Varies with state and year. Source: U.S. Department of Commerce, Bureau of the Census, Governmental Finances, selected years.
User Charges	State and local revenues from user fees and miscellaneous charges, multiplied by 100, then divided by state personal income (see above). Varies with state and year. Source: U.S. Department of Commerce, Bureau of the Census, Governmental Finances, selected years.
Corporate Tax	State corporate income tax revenues, multiplied by 100, then divided by state personal income (see above). Varies with state and year. Source: U.S. Department of Commerce, Bureau of the Census, State Government Finances, selected years.
Other Taxes	Other state and local revenues, multiplied by 100, then divided by state personal income (see above). Varies with state and year. Other revenues computed as total revenues minus property tax, sales tax, corporate tax, individual income tax revenues and user charges. Source: U.S. Department of Commerce, Bureau of the Census, Governmental Finances, selected years.
Real Transaction Value	Transaction value defined as reported total cost of the investment regardless of the source or timing of funds. Scale is tens of thousands of dollars. Value is deflated with GNP deflator for nonresidential investment. Missing values filled in, where possible, with predictions from a Box-Cox regression. Varies with investing firm. Logarithmically transformed in specifications. Source: U.S. Department of Commerce, International Trade Administration, Foreign Direct Investment in the United States, for 1978-1983, computer tape obtained from the Department of Commerce; for 1984-1987 entered from published data.
Indicator Variables	
SIC nn	Varies with investing firm. It is equal to unity if firm has two-digit SIC classification code equal to nn, and is equal to zero otherwise.
Attractiveness for SIC 28	This variable varies with state and investing firm. It is equal to unity if the firm has two-digit SIC classification code equal to 28, and the state is Alabama, Delaware, Louisiana, New Jersey, or Texas. It is equal to zero in all other cases.

Continuous variables	Description
Attractiveness for SIC 35	Varies with state and investing firm. It is equal to unity if the firm has two-digit SIC classification code equal to 35, and the state is Connecticut. It is equal to zero in all other cases.
Attractiveness for SIC 37	Varies with state and investing firm. It is equal to unity if the firm has two-digit SIC classification code equal to 37, and the state is Kentucky, Michigan, or Ohio. It is equal to zero in all other cases.
Proximity for Canada	Varies with state and investing firm. It is equal to unity if the firm is Canadian and the state shares a border with Canada, i.e., the state is Idaho, Maine, Michigan, Minnesota, Montana, New Hampshire, New York, North Dakota, Ohio, Pennsylvania, Vermont, or Washington. It is equal to zero otherwise.
Proximity for Europe	Varies with state and the investing firm. It is equal to unity if the firm is European and the state is on the eastern seaboard, i.e., the state is Connecticut, Delaware, Florida, Georgia, Maine, Maryland, Massachusetts, New Hampshire, New Jersey, New York, North Carolina, Rhode Island, South Carolina, or Virginia. It is equal to zero otherwise.
Proximity for Asia	Varies with state and investing firm. It is equal to unity if the firm is Asian and the state is on the Western seaboard, i.e., the state is California, Oregon or Washington. It is equal to zero otherwise.
Japan	Varies with investing firm. It is equal to unity if the firm is Japanese and equals zero otherwise.
United Kingdom	Varies with investing firm. It is equal to unity if the firm is from the United Kingdom and equals zero otherwise.
Other Investor	Varies with investing firm. It is equal to unity if the firm is not from Japan or the United Kingdom and is equal to zero otherwise.
Unitary	Varies with state and year. It is equal to unity if the state had a world-wide unitary tax system in place in that year, i.e., California, Idaho, Illinois, Montana and North Dakota, 1978-87; Colorado, New Hampshire, Oregon and Utah, 1978-85; Massachusetts, 1978-83; and Florida, 1983. It is equal to zero otherwise.
Europe	Varies with investing firm. It is equal to unity if the firm is European, and is equal to zero otherwise.
Asia	Varies with investing firm. It is equal to unity if the firm is Asian, and is equal to zero otherwise.

and were not statistically significant. We therefore dropped the income variables from the analysis. We believe that market variables are important to the decision to invest somewhere in the United States, but that state market variables are less important in selecting a specific location within the United States. The percentage of the workforce unionized is no longer reported on an annual basis, and our initial attempts to incorporate a unionization variable constructed from interpolation of existing data revealed little significant role for unionization.[1] We also estimated models with variables representing the state minimum wage laws and right-to-work laws, but the coefficients for these variables were also statistically insignificant. We now present the state-specific variables used in the final analyses.

Real Wage Rate

We use the state average hourly manufacturing production earnings deflated by the GNP deflator in the year that the investment is made to represent the cost of labor in the manufacturing sector for the state.[2] In preliminary analysis, the real wage rate variable performs better statistically when the values are logarithmically transformed. For a given level of productivity, we expect this variable to have a negative effect on profits, and therefore on the probability of locating in a given state.

We do not have good measures of labor productivity in each state over time, and a productivity variable is not explicitly included in the state-level analysis. To the extent that productivity of the workforce varies across regions and persists over time, the regional dummy variables that we include in the regional choice aspect of the location decision will help account for productivity differentials across regions. However, our analysis still does not account for the productivity differences among states within regions.

Employment Agglomeration

Employment agglomeration economies for manufacturers are measured as state employment in the two-digit SIC industry of the new plant as a fraction of total private employment in the state. Manufacturing firms are expected to be more attracted to states with higher concentrations of employees in their industry.

State Population

Although our employment agglomeration variable will capture the effect of the fraction of the workforce in the industry of the new plant, it will not capture the effect of the absolute size of the workforce. To this end, we included the logarithm of population in our specifications. We expect the probability of choosing a state to increase with population.

Energy Costs

Average real industrial electric energy bills in the state, deflated using the implicit GNP price index for private total consumption, were used to measure the electric costs in the state. Nominal natural gas prices per 1,000 cubic feet are deflated using the same GNP deflator as for electric bills. Both variables are logarithmically transformed in the specifications.

In preliminary runs, the energy cost variables were not statistically significant. We therefore test whether energy prices affected locations of plants for two major industry groups, Chemicals and Allied Products (SIC 28) and Primary Metals (SIC 33), that use energy intensively. Accordingly, the energy variables are interacted with two dummy variables representing these two industries. The first dummy equals unity when the new plant is built for industry group 28 and zero otherwise. The second equals unity when the new plant is built for industry group 33 and zero otherwise. We expect higher energy costs to decrease the probability of firms from these two major industry groups locating in a state.

State Attractiveness

State attractiveness is represented by a set of indicator variables meant to capture foreign industry-specific agglomeration economies and other industry-specific economies not directly related to the level of employment. A state is deemed to be attractive to a particular industry group if, out of the 1,197 original observations on new plants, it has more than eight new plants in that industry group and the number of new plants for that industry group represented more than 30 percent of the total for the time period 1978-87. This formula leads to state attractiveness indicators representing three industry groups. If a new plant for the Chemicals and Allied Products industry group is built in Alabama, Delaware, Louisiana, New Jersey, or Texas, the first indicator variable has a value of unity and a value of zero otherwise. The second indicator variable has a value of unity if the new plant is in the industry group Industrial Machinery and Equipment and the plant is located in Connecticut and has a value of zero otherwise. The third indicator variable has a value of unity, if a new plant for the industry group Transportation Equipment is built in Kentucky, Michigan, or Ohio and has a value of zero otherwise. Naturally, we expect state attractiveness to increase the probability of locating in the state.

The state attractiveness variables are our attempt to correct for so-called "spikes" in the residuals even after all the right-hand-side variables are included in the model. The corrections may appear *ad hoc* and we have not developed ironclad explanations for each of the three indicators. However, we have mentioned the tendency of Japanese firms in particular to locate near suppliers (see chapter 1) and to develop vertically integrated relationships among suppliers and between suppliers and the manufacturing assembly plant. Such practices breed regional agglomeration beyond what the standard set of state-level covariates, such as wage rates and domestic agglomeration economies, can explain. The location practices will then necessitate additional variables in the model.

At least the third indicator variable lends itself to the above explanation for the attractiveness variable. Most of the new plants in the transportation equipment major group are in the automobile manufacturing industry or are in the parts supplier aspect of that major group. The new plants are heavily concentrated in three of what Woodward (1992) names the auto-alley states—Kentucky, Michigan, and Ohio. Apparently the agglomeration variable for Transportation Equipment already included as a covariate in our model does not account fully for the heavy concentration of new foreign transportation equipment plants in these three states. We speculate that the high reliance of foreign firms on a hand-selected set of suppliers accounts for the special attractiveness of transportation equipment plants to those three states. Explanations for the other two concentrations are not as obvious to us, however.

State Proximity

Based on the location patterns examined in chapter 2, we use three sets of interactive indicator variables to capture the probable preference for states located nearer the foreign investor's home country. If the investor is a Canadian firm, the first set of indicators are unity for states bordering Canada (see table 4.1 for an exact definition), and zero otherwise. A second set of indicators have a value of unity when a European investor builds a new plant in a state on the eastern seaboard (see table 4.1 for an exact definition) and have a value of zero otherwise. The third set of indicators have a value of unity when an Asian investor builds a new plant on the western seaboard, i.e., in Washington, Oregon, or California, and are zero otherwise. We expect that the proximity of a state will increase the probability of locating there.

The state proximity variables are also somewhat *ad hoc* in nature and result from the location patterns observed in the maps in chapter 2. The question we raise is whether the location patterns are explained by the right-hand-side covariates described above and the fiscal variables that follow, or whether proximity to home country adds another dimension to the location decision.

Proximity to the home country might be important if executives regularly travel from the parent to the foreign plant. For example, an executive located at a parent corporation in Japan would fly nonstop from Tokyo to Los Angeles and take a corporate jet directly to the city elsewhere in California. The extra travel time from Los Angeles would be short. However, if the plant were located in North Carolina, the same executive flying from Tokyo would probably add at least one other commercial flight to the trip. The extra travel might take another five or six hours in the air in each direction. Moreover, the trip adds to fatigue, requires more adjustment to time zone differences, and adds probably a day to the executive's itinerary. For all those reasons, parent firms may favor locations in states that are closer to the home country, other things about equal. The same general reasoning applies to European or Canadian parent firms.

Fiscal Variables

Most research on this topic to date has included total taxes or a partial list of taxes as variables in the location models. The tax variable specification in this literature is generally an incomplete representation of the fiscal impacts of location decisions for two reasons. Firms may react differentially to various taxes, suggesting the disaggregation of the total tax variable into its component taxes. In addition, most existing empirical models either ignore the expenditure side of the budget or include only a partial list of expenditure variables. To remedy these problems, we include expenditures and taxes in the equation using state and local budget constraints. The state and local budget constraint includes expenditures, taxes, and the deficit all specified per $100 of state personal income. The budget constraint is as follows:

$$\Sigma \, EXP_i - [\Sigma \, TAXES_j + USER + AID] = DEFICIT$$

where

EXP_i = state and local expenditure per $100 of state personal income on various functions,

TAX_j = state and local tax variables per $100 of state personal income,

USER   = user charges and other revenues per $100 of state personal income,

AID   = federal aid to state and local governments in the state per $100 of state personal income, and

DEFICIT = currrent account deficit per $100 of state personal income.

The advantage of the budget constraint is that it enables us to include expenditures, taxes, user fees, intergovernmental aid, and the deficit.[3] By obtaining coefficients for each variable, we can simulate more accurately than others the effect of raising a tax or increasing expenditure. For example, a tax increase may fund an increase in expenditure or a reduction in the deficit, or an increase in intergovernmental aid can be used to reduce taxes, raise spending, or lower the deficit.

To be more specific, on the expenditure side, we include variables for health, highways, primary and secondary education, higher education, and other expenditures. On the tax side, we include variables for property, sales, individual income, corporate income, and other taxes in our empirical analysis.

A feature of the budget constraint, as it is implemented here, needs additional explanation. All of the expenditure and revenue items cannot be incorporated as right-hand-side variables into a properly identified empirical model, because the budget constraint would create exact collinearity among the fiscal variables. Therefore, we arbitrarily eliminate state and local welfare expenditures from the variables used in the empirical analysis, as do other researchers using the budget constraint.

The omission of the welfare expenditure variable affects the interpretation of the coefficients of the other fiscal variables, however. For example, an increase in a tax variable, holding all other values of the included fiscal variables constant, including the deficit, would have to be used to fund an increase in welfare expenditures. Therefore, a negative coefficient on a tax variable would mean that an increase in the tax to fund an offsetting amount of higher welfare expenditures would reduce the probability of a plant location in a state. A positive tax coefficient, on the other hand, suggests that a higher tax to fund welfare expenditures increases the probability of a foreign plant location in the state. One can also examine the effect of different combinations of tax increases and expenditure increases in nonwelfare categories of expenditure, which has the effect of holding welfare expenditure constant. For example, one can ask the effect of increasing sales taxes by $1 per $100 of personal income to reduce the deficit by $1 per $100 of personal income by comparing the coefficients on the deficit and the sales tax variables.

Corporate Tax Complications

As discussed in chapter 2, corporate taxation of multinational firms has a number of extra dimensions that we need to account for in our model. For example, corporate income taxes could have different affects on foreign plant locations when home countries operate residential as opposed to territorial tax systems. To account for the differential effects, we interact the corporate income tax variable with each of three dummy variables that represent investors from Japan, investors from the United Kingdom, and investors from other countries. Using these interaction dummies with the corporate income tax variable, we analyze whether the corporate income tax affects investors differently across countries.[4] Investors in the other country category are likely to be from countries operating territorial tax systems in which the investors pay only host country taxes. Investors from territorial-tax-system countries may be more sensitive to host country taxes than investors from countries operating a residential tax system.

The second feature of the corporate income tax variable specification involves the allocation of the firm's corporate income among the states. Firms operating plants both outside and inside of the state typically must allocate income to each state taxing entity using a formula determined by each state. States also determine the total amount of income eligible for allocation. During the 1978 to 1987 period, several states used worldwide profits as a basis for allocating income to the state (referred to above as worldwide unitary tax states). From the states' perspective, a worldwide income tax basis significantly reduces opportunities for firms to use transfer pricing to lower income subject to taxation. Firms, however, generally prefer a domestic, rather than the worldwide unitary or a domestic combination system as a basis for allocating profits to states. The empirical issue here is whether investors tend to avoid states that use worldwide unitary taxation.

To test the effect of worldwide unitary taxation, we interact the corporate income tax variable with a dummy variable representing the states with a worldwide unitary tax system in the year of the investment, and then interact the new variable with dummy variables representing the investor's home country, as above. Thus, up to three variables represent the unitary tax variable: the real corporate tax per $100 of state personal income interacted with the state unitary tax dummy interacted with Japan as the home country of the investor, the real corporate tax variable interacted with the state unitary tax dummy interacted with the United Kingdom as the home country of the investor, and the real corporate tax variable interacted with the state unitary tax dummy interacted with the indicator for another country as the home country of the investor.[5]

Region-Specific Variables

To get at regional choice, we began by grouping states into five regions, combining the Bureau of Economic Analysis region definitions in some cases. The Mountain and Pacific states—Arizona, California, Colorado, Idaho, Montana, Nevada, New Mexico, Oregon, Utah, Washington, and Wyoming—formed one region, which we called Mountain-Pacific;[6] the West South Central states—Arkansas, Louisiana, Oklahoma, and Texas—formed the second region, while the balance of the southern states—Alabama, Delaware, Florida, Georgia, Kentucky, Maryland, Mississippi, North Carolina, South Carolina, Tennessee, West Virginia, and Virginia—were grouped into a third region, which we identified as South. The New England and Middle Atlantic states—Connecticut, Maine, Massachusetts, New Hampshire, New Jersey, New York, Pennsylvania, Rhode Island, and Vermont—formed a fourth region, which we called Northeast. The East and West North Central states—Illinois, Indiana, Iowa, Kansas, Michigan, Minnesota, Missouri, Nebraska, North Dakota, Ohio, South Dakota, and Wisconsin—were grouped into a fifth region called Midwest. The Midwest region will represent the baseline region. In other words, the region-specific component of deterministic profit equals zero for the Midwest region for all years, and the region-specific component of deterministic profit for all other regions is expressed as a deviation from zero.

In the standard multinomial logit models (and the simple nested multinomial logit models) that we estimated, there are 16 variables that directly affect the choice of region, four sets of variables for each of the four regions (excluding the baseline region).[7] Three sets describe U.S. regional location interaction with the world region of the investor. The first set represents the U.S. region-specific constants, and there are four indicator variables for this set—one corresponding to each of the United States regions. In the deterministic component of profit for state s, the indicator variable corresponding to the region r in which state s is located is equal to unity, while the remaining indicators equal zero. The second set determines the differential attractiveness of the regions for European investors. The four indicator variables in this set equal the four region-specific constants when the investing firm is European, and they are all equal to zero otherwise. The third set determines the differential attractiveness of the regions for Asian investors. This case is completely analogous to the previous case, except that the indicators can be nonzero only when the investing firm is Asian. Canadian firms represent the base case, and no regional attractiveness indicators are included for Canada.

The fourth set of variables gives the effect of investment size on regional preference. The four variables here are given by the products of the logarithm of the real investment size (transaction value) with the four indicator variables defining the region-specific constants. Of the 1,195 new plants in our original data, 640 transaction values were reported. For 544 of the remaining 555 cases, predictions could be substituted from a Box-Cox regression of real transaction value on indicators for year, country of origin, and two-digit SIC code using the 640 reported values. The method used to predict the missing values is given in detail in appendix A to this chapter.

An interpretation of the coefficients for the regional variables is discussed here. For our data, we have defined three world regions as the source of new plant investments—Canada, Europe, and Asia—locating in one of the defined U.S. regions. The omitted dummy variable categories are Canada and the Midwest region of the United States. Thus, the coefficient on the variable corresponding to region r in the region-specific constant group gives the difference in profit between region r and the Midwest region for Canadian firms, holding transaction value constant. The sum of the coefficients on the constant and on the Europe dummy corresponding to region r gives the difference in profit between region r and the Midwest region for European firms, holding transaction value constant. The sum of the coefficients on the variables corresponding to region r for the constant and the Asia dummy gives the difference in profit between region r and the Midwest region for Asian firms, holding transaction value constant. Finally, the coefficient on the investment size variable corresponding to region r gives the difference in profit between region r and the Midwest region due to the logarithm of investment size for a given firm.

The results of the estimations are presented in the next section.

Results from the Standard Multinomial Logit Model

Before we move to the results proper, some preliminaries are in order. All the logit estimation in this chapter was carried out using the Davidon-Fletcher-Powell subroutine from version 3 of the GQOPT subroutine package. The computing was carried out on the IBM 3090 mainframe at Syracuse University and the IBM 3090 supercomputer at Cornell University. First and second derivatives of the log-likelihood function used in the estimation process were numerically approximated by GQOPT by means of first and second differences. The diagonal of the negative inverse of the approximated second derivative matrix provides asymptotically correct variances for the parameter estimates. Standard errors are computed as the square roots of these variances and asymptotically correct t-statistics are given by the ratio of the parameter estimate (less its hypothesized value) to the standard error. The appropriate number of degrees of freedom for the t-statistic is infinite, making our tests equivalent to the usual normal hypothesis tests where the standard errors are known.

There are two types of hypothesis tests concerning a single parameter with which we must be concerned. In the first type, we have no prior expectation about the sign of the parameter, and a two-tailed test is appropriate. In this case, whenever the t-statistic is greater than 1.96 (2.576) in absolute value, we reject the null hypothesis in favor of the alternative at the 5 percent (1 percent) level. In the second type of test, we have expectations about the sign of the parameter, and a one-tailed test is appropriate. If the estimated and anticipated signs are the same, we reject the null hypothesis in favor of the alternative at the 5 percent (1 percent) level if the absolute value of the t-statistic is greater than 1.645 (2.327). However, we do not reject the null hypothesis if the estimated sign of the parameter is different than the anticipated sign.

The final preliminary point concerns the interpretation of the parameter estimates. A positive coefficient on a given variable has the obvious interpretation of an increase in the firm's profit in a given state due to a unit increase in the given variable. Unfortunately, the profit nature of this interpretation is not very appealing; a probabilistic interpretation would be preferable. To this end, we introduce three variants of the elasticity of the state selection probability with respect to a given variable.

Strictly speaking, the elasticity of the state selection probability with respect to a given continuous variable is defined to be the percentage change in the state selection probability due to a 1 percent change in the continuous variable. We use this definition of elasticity when the continuous variable is logarithmically transformed in the deterministic component of profit, calling it a Type I elasticity. Then, if we denote the continuous variable by x, its associated coefficient by γ and the state selection probability by P_q, the Type I elasticity is given by

$$\varepsilon_x = \gamma(1 - P_q) \tag{4.1}$$

in the standard multinomial logit model. Unfortunately, when the continuous variable is not logarithmically transformed, the Type I definition of elasticity entails an expression that depends on the value of x. In the case where the continuous variable is not logarithmically transformed, we shall define the selection probability elasticity to be the percentage change in the state selection probability due to a unit change in x. We shall call this a Type II elasticity. The formula for the Type II elasticity in the standard multinomial logit model is identical to that of the Type I elasticity in equation (4.1). The last case to be considered is when x is an indicator (dummy-type) variable. In this case, interpretations based on derivatives are not possible. If we let P_q^1 denote the value of the state selection probability when the indicator is unity and P_q^0 the value of the probability when the indicator is zero, our Type III elasticity is defined to be the difference P_q^1 minus P_q^0, as a proportion of P_q^0. The formula for this elasticity is

$$\varepsilon_x = (\exp(\gamma) - 1)(1 - P_q^1) \tag{4.2}$$

in the standard multinomial logit model.[8] It remains to choose values at which to evaluate the state selection probabilities. One reasonable value is the reciprocal of 48 (0.021), the theoretical mean value of the probability. A second reasonable value is the sample mean probability for California. Of the 1,184 new plants in our sample, 120 are located in California, giving a sample proportion of 0.101. Other values will be introduced as they are used.

Which Logit Model

Our specification search started with the standard multinomial logit and simple nested multinomial logit models that incorporated all of the state-specific variables (including the variables for proximity to home country or continent) and the region-specific variables for four of the five regions constructed. In both the multinomial logit and simple nested logit models, the proximity variables performed strongly and indicated that proximity was a positive attractive force. However, in the simple nested logit model, the estimated value of the common dissimilarity parameter exceeded unity and therefore violated the Daly-Zachary-McFadden condition for consistency with stochastic profit maximization. The amount that the dissimilarity parameter exceeded unity decreased when the proximity variables were dropped from the analysis. Accordingly, we decided to delete the proximity variables from the generalized nested multinomial logit specifications that we attempted. The results from the generalized nested multinomial logit specifications suggested a model in which California was separated from the Mountain-Pacific region (see appendix A to this chapter for more details). Because the added complexity of the region-specific dissimilarity parameters detracted from the explanatory power of the covariates, we returned finally to the standard multinomial logit model. The nested logit results also suggested that the IIA assumption was not violated and the standard multinomial logit model is appropriate for estimating our model.

The mean values of the right-hand-side covariates are listed in table 4.2. We can now analyze the empirical results for the standard multinomial logit model, which are presented in table 4.3. The column labeled Model I contains the results for the preferred specification in which California has been removed from the Mountain-Pacific region and the column labeled Model II contains the results in the case where California is included in the Mountain-Pacific region.

Wage Rates and Energy Costs

The wage rate variable and the four energy cost variables performed rather poorly in both Models I and II. Several of these variables did well, however, in several preliminary specifications of the estimation models in which we included fewer right-hand-side covariates. All of

Table 4.2 Selected Variable Means Over the Period 1987-1987

	California	New York	Overall
Real Wage (real dollars/hour)	9.017	8.447	8.309
Population (millions)	25.102	17.686	4.809
Real Electric Bill (real dollars)	4,250.024	6,781.861	3,648.287
Real Gas Bill (real dollars/1000 cubic feet)	4.036	4.279	3.657
Intergovernmental Aid (cents/dollar state personal income)	3.292	4.209	3.732
Deficit (cents/dollar state personal income)	-0.878	-1.397	-0.953
Health Expenditures (cents/dollar state personal income)	1.394	2.028	1.477
Highway Expenditures (cents/dollar state personal income)	0.767	1.164	1.778
Primary and Secondary Education Expenditures (cents/dollar state personal income)	3.563	4.608	4.294
Higher Education Expendiutres (cents/dollar state personal income)	1.709	1.156	1.779
Other Expenditures (cents/dollar state personal income)	6.272	8.460	5.955
Property Tax (cents/dollar state personal income)	2.793	4.618	3.153
Sales Tax (cents/dollar state personal income)	2.838	2.754	2.331
Individual Income Tax (cents/dollar state personal income)	2.327	3.424	1.634
User Charges (cents/dollar state personal income)	3.588	3.637	4.273
Corporate Tax (cents/dollar state personal income)	0.877	0.669	0.461
Other Taxes (cents/dollar state personal income)	1.463	3.000	2.557

Table 4.3 Comparison of Two Sets of Multinomial Logit Results for State and Region Choice by Foreign Investors: 1978-1987

Variables	Estimates	
	Model I	Model II
General State Variables:		
Log Real Wage	-0.402	-0.349
	(-0.873)	(-0.763)
Employment Agglomeration	15.121	15.003
	(6.445)	(6.449)
Log Population	1.165	1.131
	(14.672)	(15.909)
Log Real Electric Bill x SIC 28	-0.557	-0.667
	(-1.567)	(-1.834)
Log Real Electric Bill x SIC 33	0.475	0.405
	(0.769)	(0.682)
Log Real Gas Bill x SIC 28	0.133	0.142
	(0.307)	(0.327)
Log Real Gas Bill x SIC 33	-0.562	-0.609
	(-0.609)	(-0.784)
Attractiveness for SIC 28	1.337	1.342
	(7.032)	(7.016)
Attractiveness for SIC 35	1.691	1.656
	(5.548)	(5.490)
Attractiveness for SIC 37	1.894	1.906
	(8.718)	(8.792)
State Fiscal Variables:		
Intergovernmental Aid	0.301	0.270
	(2.502)	(2.339)
Deficit	-0.389	-0.432
	(-2.770)	(-3.223)
Health Expenditures	0.151	0.204
	(0.826)	(1.162)
Highway Expenditures	-0.315	-0.271
	(-1.694)	(-1.497)
Primary and Secondary Education Expenditures	-0.257	-0.176
	(-1.434)	(-1.085)
Higher Education Expenditures	0.685	0.693
	(3.550)	(3.563)
Other Expenditures	0.029	0.070
	(0.191)	(0.475)

Variables	Estimates	
	Model I	Model II
Property Tax	-0.035	-0.061
	(-0.255)	(-0.447)
Sales Tax	-0.155	-0.190
	(-1.160)	(-1.470)
Individual Income Tax	-0.105	-0.141
	(-0.826)	(-1.147)
User Charges	-0.343	-0.399
	(-2.034)	(-2.508)
Corporate Tax	-0.579	-0.669
	(-2.581)	(-3.155)
Corporate Tax x Unitary	-0.265	-0.360
	(-1.111)	(-1.631)
Other Taxes	-0.219	-0.247
	(-1.508)	(-1.739)
Regional Variables:		
Mountain Pacific		
Constant	-0.289	0.693
	(-0.326)	(1.020)
Europe	-1.146	-1.251
	(-2.015)	(-2.689)
Asia	-0.956	-0.455
	(-1.694)	(-0.998)
Log Real Transaction Value	0.260	0.065
	(2.263)	(0.772)
West South Central		
Constant	-0.805	-0.811
	(-0.922)	(-0.951)
Europe	-0.246	-0.241
	(-0.407)	(-0.411)
Asia	-0.522	-0.518
	(-0.851)	(-0.868)
Log Real Transaction Value	0.204	0.198
	(1.946)	(1.898)
South		
Constant	1.872	1.865
	(3.226)	(3.125)
Europe	-0.459	-0.460
	(-1.200)	(-1.157)

| Variables | Estimates | |
	Model I	Model II
Asia	-1.222	-1.223
	(-3.081)	(-2.992)
Log Real Transaction Value	-0.057	-0.059
	(-0.762)	(-0.799)
Northeast		
Constant	3.650	3.645
	(6.008)	(5.747)
Europe	-1.024	-1.026
	(-2.666)	(-2.575)
Asia	-1.996	-2.005
	(-4.945)	(-4.760)
Log Real Transaction Value	-0.300	-0.299
	(-3.542)	(-3.533)
California		
Constant	1.107	--
	(1.461)	
Europe	-1.340	--
	(-2.558)	
Asia	-0.143	--
	(-0.283)	
Log Real Transaction Value	-0.057	--
	(-0.573)	
Log-Likelihood	-3816.52	-3823.98

*t-statistics in parentheses.

these were expected to have negative coefficients, but none was significant even at the 5 percent level. (In fact, the coefficient on the real electric bill is significant at the 5 percent level for firms with two-digit SIC code 28, Chemicals and Allied Products, in Model II and almost significant at that level in Model I.)

There are at least a couple of reasons for this generally poor statistical performance. First, a higher wage rate is likely to deter state selection only when labor productivity is held equal. Unfortunately, while our regional indicator variables account for productivity differences among regions, our only measure of productivity differences among states is rather indirect—state expenditures on higher education (relative to state personal income) at the time of the investment. This may be an insufficient control for productivity differences. In our review of the literature (chapter 2), we found the evidence mixed on whether wage rates affect location decisions. In fact, other research on FDI location has infrequently found wages a significant determinant of location. The domestic location literature produces more mixed results for wages.

For the energy cost variables, at least part of the problem may be that we have only electric bill information and not costs per unit of electricity. The electric bill information will be a less appropriate measure of energy prices to the extent that the composition of energy-intensive manufacturing firms varies across states. Locations of energy-intensive plants would theoretically be more sensitive to higher state energy prices than other plants. Nonetheless, energy costs are less important as location determinants generally in research done on location choices in 1980 or later.

Employment Agglomeration and State Population

The results for industry-specific employment agglomeration and the logarithm population are extremely strong in both Models I and II. For Model I, holding employment agglomeration constant, the Type I elasticity for population is 1.141 evaluated at the mean probability of 0.021 and 1.047 evaluated at the sample proportion for California. On the other hand, holding population constant, the Type II elasticity of industry-specific employment agglomeration is 14.806 at the mean probability and 13.588 at the value for California. The calculations are similar for Model II. These findings are consistent with other research on the locations of both domestic and foreign manufacturing plants. In addition to a suggestion that plants find advantages in locations at which other plants in its industry group have located, the findings reinforce the view that foreign plants tend to locate in states that already have a higher concentration of industry in their major group, especially for the four industries that dominate the new foreign manufacturing plants in our sample. Thus, foreign plants tend to build on the traditional strengths in the state. However, those traditional industries may be declining or growing within the state; our research sheds little light on the issue of whether foreign plants replace declining industries or compete with domestic growth industries. The answer to that question is likely to vary by industry with Transportation Equipment and Industrial Equipment yielding different results.

State Attractiveness

All three state attractiveness variables have positive coefficients that are statistically significant at the 1 percent level in both Models I and II. Type III elasticities for these variables give the percentage difference in the selection probability in moving from an industry that is not specially attracted to the state to an industry that is. Texas held a special attraction for the Chemicals and Allied Products (SIC 28) group. In our sample, the sample proportion for a firm choosing Texas was 88/1184 or 0.074. Accordingly, the Type III elasticity for the Chemicals and Allied Products group, evaluated at the sample proportion for Texas, is 1.238. Connecticut was attractive to the Industrial Machinery and Equipment (SIC 35) group. Our sample proportion for a firm choosing Connecticut was 39/1184 or 0.033. This value implies a Type III elasticity for the Industrial Machinery and Equipment group of 1.635 when evaluated at the value for Connecticut. Finally, Michigan was especially attractive to the Transportation Equipment group (SIC 37). The sample proportion for a firm choosing Michigan was 31/1184 or 0.026. This value gives rise to a Type III elasticity for the Transportation Equipment group of 1.844, when evaluated at the Michigan value. As discussed earlier, these variables were added to account for spikes in our distribution of residuals in initial multinomial logit runs. We believe that the variables account for agglomeration economies and location practices related to vertical integration of manufacturing at different plants that are not captured in our more traditional agglomeration economy measure.

Fiscal Variables

Some of the tax and expenditure variables are significant at the 5 percent level. Excluding for the moment the corporate tax variables, we find, for both Models I and II, statistical significance in the expected direction for intergovernmental aid, the deficit variable, and higher education expenditures at the 1 percent level, and for user charges at the 5 percent level. In Model II only, other taxes are significant at the 5 percent level in the expected direction. The case of highway expenditures is moot. To the extent that highway expenditures are considered beneficial like any other expenditures, we would expect its associated coefficient to be positive. However, to the extent that higher expenditures on highways reflect a general state of disrepair, we might expect the coefficient to be negative. The coefficient for highway expenditures in Model I is negative and significant at the 10 percent level based on a two-tailed test.

Evaluating at the mean probability 0.021, the relevant Type II elasticities in Model I are 0.295 for intergovernmental aid, -0.381 for a deficit increase, 0.671 for an increase in higher education expenditures, and -0.336 for an increase in user charges, while the Type II elasticity for other taxes in Model II is -0.242. Evaluating at the sample proportion for California, 0.101, the elasticities in Model I are 0.270 for intergovernmental aid, -0.350 for the deficit, 0.616 for higher education expenditures, and -0.308 for user charges; the elasticity value for other taxes in Model II is -0.222. The values for higher education expenditures are both quite high, and demonstrate the concern foreign investors have for future productivity of the workforce.

Corporate Taxes

Of the two corporate tax variables in each of our final models, the amount of corporate tax revenue as a proportion of state personal income is significant at the 1 percent level in both Models I and II. The Type II elasticity of the corporate tax in Model I is -0.567, evaluated at the mean probability. Evaluating at the sample proportion for California (and including the unitary tax system coefficient), the elasticity reaches -0.758. The large effect of corporate taxes on location is surprising in light of other foreign plant location studies that find only weak (at best) locational effects for the corporate tax variable. Our more complete specification of the government's budget constraint and the addition of expenditure and taxes in a consistent manner apparently improved on the estimation precision for the effects of fiscal variables on the location of foreign plants. The lack of significance for the unitary tax system variables (even though it is close to significant at the 5 percent level in Model II) indicates that foreign firms were not uniformly concerned about this aspect of the tax system throughout the 1978-87 period. Because plants locate in areas for what is expected to be the long run, the reduction in the number of states using the worldwide unitary tax system during the 1980s appears to have reduced its significance as a location deterrent, compared to the findings of other studies.

Bar charts for the elasticities for the state-specific covariates are presented in figures 4.1 and 4.2. Figure 4.1 contains the results evaluated at the mean probability 0.021, while the results are evaluated at the sample proportion for California in figure 4.2.

Region-Specific Variables

In preliminary analysis, we included the state proximity variables discussed earlier in the specifications, and they were always significant at the 5 percent level. As explained above, these variables were removed from the final analysis because the determination of proximity is somewhat arbitrary and because they resulted in estimates of dissimilarity parameters that were not consistent with stochastic profit maximization. When state proximity variables were included in the preliminary specifications, regional preferences inferred from the region-specific variables would be interpreted as being net of effects due to proximity. When, in the final analysis, state proximity variables are excluded from the specification, regional preferences inferred from the region-specific variables include effects due to proximity.

Turning first to the log real transaction value variable, we note that the associated coefficient for the Northeast is negative and significant at the 1 percent level in both Model I and Model II, indicating again

Figure 4.1 Tax Elasticities for Mean State Selection Probabili

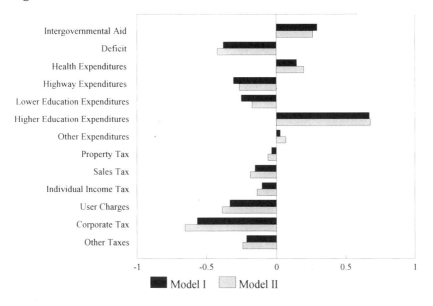

Figure 4.2 Tax Elasticities for California Selection Probability

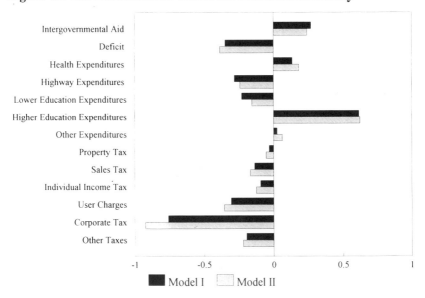

that larger investments from all world regions have a higher probability of locating in the Midwest (the excluded indicator variable category) than in the Northeast. For example, the sample proportion for firms locating in New York is 81/1184 or 0.068. But the Type I elasticity with respect to the real transaction value for locating in New York is -0.279. In California, on the other hand, for Model I (with California separated from the Mountain-Pacific region) the transaction value coefficient is significantly positive at the 5 percent level for the Mountain-Pacific region. The finding indicates that larger investments are more attracted to the Mountain-Pacific region, excluding California, than the Midwest region. The sample proportion for firms locating in Washington State is 23/1184 or 0.019. Accordingly, the Type I elasticity with respect to the real transaction value for locating in Washington is 0.255.

The region-specific constants are significant consistently across models I and II. In general, firms prefer the South and Northeast to other regions of the United States, when transaction values are held constant. European firms prefer the Midwest to the Northeast, the Mountain-Pacific, and California regions, holding real transaction value constant. European firms are indifferent between the Midwest region and the remaining southern regions of the United States. Asian firms tend to avoid the Northeast and the South compared to the Midwest as locations, all else equal. Moreover, these results suggest Asian investors have no particular preferences for California over the Midwest. That result is somewhat surprising in light of our observation in chapter 2 that Japanese manufacturing was heavily concentrated in California during the 1978 to 1987 period. However, given the empirical results reported here, we are led to conclude that once agglomeration economies, population, wage and energy costs, and fiscal variables are accounted for, there is little over and above these that Asian firms find attractive in California.

Predictive Ability

In the next chapter we use the coefficient results from Model I to perform simulation experiments in which we estimate the effects of changing policy variables on the probability of locating in a particular state. We perform the simulations using the data for the entire 1978 to

1987 period of analysis, for 1979, and for 1987. However, before we examine state-specific results from simulations, it is useful to know how well the estimated model predicts location outcomes or probabilities of location in various states.

To judge the predictive precision of the estimated model, we compare the model's predicted values for states to the baseline or actual probabilities. The baseline is calculated for 1979, for example, as the actual percentages of the 173 total foreign manufacturing plants in 1979 that located in each state. Thus, the baseline percentages should sum to 100. Analogous methods are used to estimate baseline location percentages for each state in 1987 and for the overall sample. We then difference the model's predicted percentage of firms locating in each state and the baseline figure for each state to obtain the prediction error. A positive value for the prediction error means that the model overpredicts the frequency with which firms select the given state during the given time period, while a negative value for the prediction error means that the model underpredicts the same frequency.

One striking feature of the results, which are presented in table 4.4 (with outliers offset from the column of numbers under the heading "prediction error"), is that, for the entire sample period, states with the highest sample proportions (actual percentage) have the lowest relative prediction errors, where relative prediction error is defined as the prediction error divided by the actual percentage. This occurs because the maximum likelihood estimation technique produces the best fit overall by fitting the states with the highest sample proportions most exactly. It is for this reason that California, which has the highest actual percentage over the period 1978-1987, has a prediction error close to 0 percent. The states with the three next highest actual percentages, Texas, North Carolina, and New York, also have small relative prediction errors for the period 1978-1987.

The first exception is Georgia, the state with the fifth highest actual percentage. For the period 1978-1987, the model underpredicts the relative frequency for Georgia by close to 2.5 percentage points. The only other state with an underprediction of more than 1 percentage point for the entire sample period is Connecticut. We may conclude that Georgia and Connecticut hold a special attraction to foreign firms building new plants that is not captured by our covariates. Turning to overpredictions of the relative frequency, two southern states, Florida and Mississippi, are among the three states with overpredictions of more than 1 percent for the entire sample period (the third state is Massachusetts). One possible explanation for the results for Florida and Mississippi is the omission in our model of controls for interracial relations, and possibly crime associated with a pervasive underclass.

If the relative frequency for a state is substantially overpredicted (underpredicted) over the entire sample period, then it is reasonable to expect that their actual percentages will be overpredicted in each of the years 1979 and 1987. In fact, this pattern holds for all three southern states mentioned—Georgia, Florida, and Mississippi. For Georgia, there are underpredictions in excess of 3 percentage points in both 1979 and 1987. For both Florida and Mississippi, there are overpredictions in excess of 1.5 percentage points in each of 1979 and 1987. In the case of Massachusetts, the prediction error is moderate (if not small) for 1979, but is greater than 2 percentage points for 1987. Although it is not the only conclusion consistent with the prediction error pattern for Massachusetts, one strongly suspects that the quality of the predictions for Massachusetts deteriorate as the sample period progresses.

There is a final possibility that should be examined. A state might have a relatively low absolute prediction error over the entire period, yet have a relatively high absolute prediction error in each of the two years we examine. There are two reasons that this might occur. The first reason is a naturally high variance for the prediction error of a given state. The second possible reason is the omission of economic factors from the model that might distinguish the state of affairs in the early part of the period, when the economy performed relatively poorly, from the state of affairs in the latter part of the period, when the economy performed relatively well. If the second reason is to be considered valid for a particular state, we would almost certainly expect the prediction errors to be of opposite signs in 1979 and 1987. Of the seven states not yet mentioned in this analysis that have prediction errors greater than 1 percent in absolute value in both years, the pattern of a sign switch holds for six of them: California, Connecticut, Delaware, Louisiana, Ohio, and Texas. Only Pennsylvania, which had positive prediction errors in excess of 2 percentage points in 1979 and 1987, did not have a sign switch.

Table 4.4 Analysis of Prediction Errors for Model I (outliers offset to right of column)

State	Overall Actual percentage	Overall Prediction error	1979 Actual percentage	1979 Prediction error	1987 Actual percentage	1987 Prediction error
Alabama	2.524	0.947	2.312	1.852	3.521	0.608
Arizona	0.591	0.198	0.578	0.597	0.000	0.450
Arkansas	0.507	0.390	1.734	-0.714	0.000	0.736
California	10.135	0.000	80.92	-1.816	9.155	2.981
Colorado	0.571	0.519	0.000	1.488	0.704	0.250
Connecticut	3.294	-1.005	4.624	-2.057	0.000	1.571
Delaware	0.760	0.240	0.578	1.187	1.408	-0.996
Florida	2.196	2.292	2.890	1.955	0.000	3.101
Georgia	6.672	-2.481	9.827	-5.106	6.338	-3.458
Idaho	0.000	0.322	0.000	0.296	0.000	0.493
Illinois	4.139	-0.416	2.890	0.408	7.042	-3.044
Indiana	2.534	-0.301	1.734	0.645	7.042	-4.107
Iowa	0.422	0.093	0.000	0.393	0.704	0.394
Kansas	0.084	0.313	0.000	0.422	0.704	-0.181
Kentucky	2.534	-0.396	1.156	0.257	4.225	-2.007
Louisiana	1.182	-0.300	3.468	-1.932	0.000	1.635
Maine	0.507	-0.021	1.156	-0.654	0.000	0.446
Maryland	1.858	0.159	1.156	0.701	0.704	1.969
Massachusetts	2.027	1.148	2.890	0.000		2.322
Michigan	2.618	0.700	1.734	0.898	4.930	-0.956
Minnesota	0.760	-0.238	1.734	-1.134	0.000	0.625
Mississippi	0.591	1.258	0.000	2.222	0.000	1.791
Missouri	1.744	-0.213	0.578	0.897	0.704	0.973

Montana	0.000	0.085	0.000	0.117		0.000	0.087	
Nebraska	0.084	0.189	0.578	-0.289		0.000	0.421	
Nevada	0.253	-0.156	0.000	0.135		1.408		-1.276
New Hampshire	0.169	0.124	0.578	-0.297		0.000	0.362	
New Jersey	3.176	-0.213	2.890	0.386		3.521	-0.316	
New Mexico	0.338	-0.134	0.000	0.340		0.000	0.104	
New York	6.841	-0.220	4.046		5.557	4.225	0.823	
North Carolina	7.517	-0.920	5.202	-0.101		7.042	-0.370	
North Dakota	0.084	-0.039	0.000	0.030		0.000	0.065	
Ohio	4.054	-0.360	1.156		1.993	9.155		-3.524
Oklahoma	0.338	0.484	0.578	0.442		0.704	-0.081	
Oregon	1.436	-0.698	0.578	0.093		3.521		-2.187
Pennsylvania	2.956	0.886	1.734		2.003	0.704		2.455
Rhode Island	0.676	-0.162	1.734		-1.026	1.408		-1.056
South Carolina	3.041	0.183	5.202		-1.570	2.817	-0.203	
South Dakota	0.084	0.003	0.578	-0.463		0.000	0.070	
Tennessee	4.307	-0.988	4.046		-1.213	7.042		-3.884
Texas	7.432	-0.574	11.561		-4.028	3.521		1.968
Utah	0.422	0.188	1.156	-0.580		0.000	0.985	
Vermont	0.929	-0.519	1.734		-1.290	0.704	-0.538	
Virginia	3.547	-0.205	5.202		-2.459	3.521	-0.085	
Washington	1.943	-0.400	1.734	-0.004		2.113	0.691	
West Virginia	0.507	-0.088	0.578	-0.159		0.000	0.327	
Wisconsin	1.014	0.270	0.000		1.162	1.408	-0.440	
Wyoming	0.000	0.076	0.000	0.155		0.000	0.019	

It is hard to suggest definite criteria for an acceptable level of predictive power for a model. The most one can hope for is an insight into the possible deficiencies of a model. Our preferred model seriously overpredicts for two states with high racial tensions and/or a high crime rate, Florida and Mississippi. It also demonstrates a high prediction error variance (that may or may not be related to changing economic conditions over the sample period) for eight other states: California, Connecticut, Delaware, Louisiana, Massachusetts, Ohio, Pennsylvania, and Texas.

Summary And Conclusions

In the previous studies on business location decisions, both generally and specifically those that restricted their attention to activity by foreign firms, there has been little consensus on the determinants of these decisions. Conclusions concerning the effects of wages, energy costs, and local tax structure have been mixed. There is considerable agreement that agglomeration is an important factor in determining where businesses locate.

In this chapter, we have empirically examined which factors determine the state location of new plants built by foreign firms. Using standard and nested multinomial logit analysis, we estimated several specifications and variants on a data set collected by the International Trade Administration of the U.S. Department of Commerce, spanning the period from 1978 to 1987. Our results indicate that wage rates and energy costs are not important determinants of the location decision, although we acknowledge that these results may be artifacts of insufficient productivity controls for labor productivity in the first case and unreliable electricity cost data in the second case. As in previous studies, we found agglomeration to be important, but also discovered a strong effect for the absolute population level.

We found that investors from certain world regions eschewed particular regions of the United States, apparently because of the distances between them. In preliminary analysis, we did, however, find proximity to be an important determinant of the location decision, but noted that including proximity variables exacerbated the problem of satisfying the technical condition of consistency with stochastic utility maximization in the nested logits. In the nested logit framework, we found evidence to suggest that California should be considered its own region and that there may be problems attendant with grouping all the states from the New England and Middle Atlantic Census regions into a single region for purposes of analysis.

We move finally to our results for state fiscal structure. We found several components of state revenues and state expenditures to be important determinants of where the foreign firms locate their new plants. Higher deficits were a negative factor. Particularly important on the expenditure side was higher education, reflecting firms' interest in maintaining or increasing labor productivity. On the revenue side, higher user charges worked significantly against state selection. Foreign firms also reacted negatively to higher corporate income taxes. On the other hand, worldwide unitary tax systems in the host state were not an important negative factor.

In the next chapter, we simulate the effects of changes in state policy on the number of foreign firms that choose to locate new plants in that state.

Appendix A to Chapter 4

Box-Cox Estimation of Missing Real Transaction Values

As discussed in the text, 555 of our remaining 1,195 observations in the ITA data have missing values for the real transaction value or the real amount of the investment. We use a Box-Cox method to estimate an equation from which to predict the missing real transaction values.

The Box-Cox regression methodology, developed by Box and Cox (1964), uses a power transformation for the dependent variable to allow a flexible functional form on the left-hand-side of a regression. The power transformation requires the estimation of a transformation parameter λ together with the linear coefficient vector β and the disturbance variance σ^2. Thus, instead of the usual normal linear regression model

$$y_i = \beta_0 + X_{1i}\beta_1 + X_{2i}\beta_2 + \dots + X_{ki}\beta_k + \varepsilon_i,$$ (4A.1)

where y_i is the dependent variable for individual i, the $X_{\cdot i}$'s are a collection of regressors, the β_i's are elements of β, and ε_i is the normal disturbance, the Box-Cox regression methodology estimates

$$(y_i^\lambda - 1) / \lambda = \beta_0 + X_{1i}\beta_1 + X_{2i}\beta_2 = \dots + X_{ki}B_k + \varepsilon_i.$$ (4A.2)

The Box-Cox transformation parameter λ can be any real number. It produces a linear regression when $\lambda = 1$, and as λ limits to zero, the left-hand-side of equation (4A.2), call it $y_i^{(\lambda)}$, limits to $\ln(y_i)$ so that a semilog regression results. Because of this flexibility for the functional form of the left-hand-side, the Box-Cox regression methodology is an excellent tool for prediction when the functional form of the left-hand-side is unknown.[9] In the application described above, we estimated λ, β and σ^2 using the NLIN procedure from version 5 of the SAS programming language on the IBM 3090 at Syracuse University using the 640 cases for which the real transaction value (y_i) was known. (The sample mean of the real transaction value over these 640 cases was $26,542,500.) (See table 4A.1.) For the 544 cases for which the real transaction value was missing but could be predicted, we used β and the appropriate values of the $X_{\cdot i}$'s for that observation to predict the left-hand-side of equation (4A.2), $y_i^{(\lambda)}$. The value for the real transaction value y_i can now be computed using the inverse Box-Cox transformation

$$y_i = (\lambda y_i^{(\lambda)} + 1)^{(1/\lambda)}.$$ (4A.3)

In our multinomial logit analysis, we used the actual value of the real transaction value for the 640 observations for which it was available, and the predicted value for the 544 cases for which a prediction was possible. The remaining cases were dropped. The sample mean, over the 1,184 cases, of the real transaction value used in our analysis was $18,377,500.

Table 4A.1 Box-Cox Parameter Estimates for Prediction of Real Transaction Value

	Value		Value
Transformation Parameter	0.013	**Year Indicator**	
Intercept	-0.593	1979	0.258
Country Indicator		1980	-0.018
Australia	-1.190	1981	0.027
Austria	-0.542	1982	-0.329
Belgium	-0.114	1983	-0.465
Canada	-1.258	1984	0.271
China	-1.102	1985	0.199
Denmark	-0.748	1986	0.3 42
France	-0.397	1987	0.326
Germany	-0.246	**SIC Code Indicator**	
Greece	-0.016	SIC 20	0.994
Ireland	-1.047	SIC 22	0.736
Israel	-0.638	SIC 23	0.642
Italy	-0.749	SIC 24	0.003
Korea	-0.403	SIC 25	-0.026
Liechtenstein	0.750	SIC 26	1.108
Netherlands	-0.463	SIC 27	0.355
New Zealand	-0.251	SIC 28	0.991
Norway	-0.425	SIC 29	1.704
Saudi Arabia	1.707	SIC 30	0.112
Spain	0.253	SIC 31	0.600
Sweden	0.101	SIC 3 2	0.929
Switzerland	-0.099	SIC 33	1.379
Taiwan	-0.555	SIC 34	0.214
United Kingdom	0.133	SIC 35	0.190
Yugoslavia	-3.038	SIC 36	0.995
		SIC 37	0.973
		SIC 38	0.094

Appendix B to Chapter 4

The purpose of this appendix is to provide the reader with a comprehensive account of the specification search that we conducted involving the standard multinomial logit, simple nested multinomial logit, and generalized nested multinomial models. The search included specifications for the simple and generalized nested multinomial logit models with the complete set of state-specific covariates involved in the estimation of the preferred standard multinomial logit models (Models I and II) presented in the main text. However, the specification search also included specifications for all three variants of the multinomial logit model on a wider set of state-specific covariates than that used for Models I and II.

The widest set of state-specific covariates used in the specification search extended to two types of state-specific covariates discussed in chapter 4. The first type comprised the state proximity variables. The second type comprised the interaction of the pure corporate tax variable with indicators for Japan, the United Kingdom and Other Investors, and the interaction of the corporate tax variable for worldwide unitary states with the same three indicators. Thus, instead of two corporate tax variables as in Models I and II, the specifications with the widest set of state-specific variables had six corporate tax variables.

In the standard multinomial logit model, the three proximity variables all had positive coefficients statistically significant at the 5 percent level. The same thing was true in the simple nested multinomial logit model. However, the performance of the six tax variables in the standard and simple nested multinomial logit models was not as convincing as the performance of the proximity variables. In the standard multinomial logit model, the only one of the six that was significant at the 5 percent significance level was the pure variable interacted with the indicator for Japan. Using a likelihood ratio test in the simple nested multinomial logit specification, we could not reject the null hypothesis that the coefficients on the pure corporate tax variables were different across the three country groups or that the coefficients on the corporate tax variables for worldwide unitary states were different across the three country groups.

In all our specifications using the simple nested multinomial logit model, the estimates for the dissimilarity parameter exceeded unity and therefore violated the Daly-Zachary-McFadden condition for consistency with stochastic profit maximization. Moreover, they also almost certainly violate Börsch-Supan's proposed relaxation of the Daly-Zachary-McFadden condition.

Although the dissimilarity parameter estimates were insignificantly different from unity at all conventional significance levels, obvious methodological problems would arise if we attempted to use the point estimates from these models in simulation experiments. We therefore felt it necessary to examine the generalized nested multinomial logit model.

It seemed appropriate, before we started our analysis with the generalized nested logit, to choose a baseline specification for the analysis. In doing this, we noted that the simple nested logit models without the state proximity variables produced the lower estimates for the dissimilarity parameter. Given this fact, together with the poor general performance of the tax variables differing by home country, we chose a set of state-specific covariates that did not include the proximity variables and did not allow the tax variables to differ by home country.

The results for the generalized nested multinomial logit model are presented in table 4B.1. Model III presents the results for the baseline specification with a distinct value for the dissimilarity parameter for each of the five regions. An examination of the dissimilarity parameter estimates indicates that the problems arise with the Mountain-Pacific and Northeast regions, where the estimates are 1.440 and 1.677, respectively, and the latter is significantly different from unity. This suggests that California and New York do not belong with the smaller states in their respective regions. To investigate this possibility, we estimated Model IV, in which California and New York represent separate regions. (In so doing, we normalized the dissimilarity parameters for the new California and New York regions to equal unity, since these parameters are not otherwise identified.) The results for Model IV were better for the Mountain-Pacific dissimilarity parameter (1.011) and for the Northeast dissimilarity parameter, which is no longer significantly different from unity.

Although the Model IV variant of the analysis appears to have solved the important problems facing us, there are at least two reasons why we did not want to end with this specification. First, it did not seem completely appropriate to include New York in a region by itself, since both Texas and North Carolina received more new plants than New York. Second, standard errors for the coefficient estimates increased substantially over Model III, especially on the tax and expenditure variables.

In Model V, we divided the Northeast into its two Census regions, New England and Middle Atlantic. This estimation only exacerbated the problem—the dissimilarity parameter estimate for the New England region, which includes New York, increased in value to 1.993. In a further estimation (not shown in table 4A.1), we again divided the Northeast into two regions, the first made up of New York, Pennsylvania, New Jersey, and Connecticut and the second containing the remaining Northeastern states. The same type of problem arose.

Accordingly, we decided on a final generalized nested multinomial logit estimation, in which six regions were specified—the original five with California excluded from the Mountain-Pacific and becoming its own region. The results are presented in Model VI. The dissimilarity parameter estimate for the Mountain-Pacific region came out to be 1.101, down from the value of 1.440 in Model III. For the Northeast, the estimate was down to 1.600. This is the lowest value of the models considered in this analysis, and unlike the result in Model III it is insignificantly different from unity. Still, the point estimate clearly violates Börsch-Supan's (1990) necessary condition. Moreover, even in this model there is an increased lack of precision in the coefficient estimates, especially for the corporate tax rate variables. We were led to conclude that it may be impossible to estimate precisely both the coefficients and the dissimilarity parameters. Still there was a lesson to be learned from our investigation—it is important to separate California from the Mountain-Pacific region in the estimation.

NOTES

1. Curme, Hirsch, and MacPherson (1990) have used data from the Current Population Survey to construct the proportion of unionized workers in the private and public sectors by state for the 1983 through the 1988 period. That data combined with earlier estimates from the same data source represents a continuous data series of the proportion of the private sector workforce that is unionized by state. However, neither series has the percentage of workers unionized in the manufacturing sector. We believe that using the total unionized workforce in the manufacturing and nonmanufacturing sectors as a proxy variable for unionization in the manufacturing sector would subject our results to severe measurement error. We, therefore, did not include the union variable in our analysis. In addition, though, regional dummy variables included in the analysis may help to capture variations in workforce unionization among regions of the United States.

2. Real values are commonly used in analysis across time to account for the affects of inflation or prices. By deflating, we remove the effects of general price increases.

3. Helms (1985) was the first person to include taxes and spending in his empirical work using the state and local government budget constraint.

4. For a discussion of residential, territorial, and mixed tax systems used in various countries, see our discussion in chapter 1 and Slemrod (1989).

5. In chapter 2, we noted that the domestic unitary states coincided to some extent with the states that receive no foreign investment. Because we believe that a domestic unitary tax dummy variable would pick up the effect of other undesirable factors in these states rather than the effect of a domestic unitary tax, we have excluded the variable from our model.

6. California was excluded from the Mountain-Pacific region in our preferred specification.

7. In our preferred specification, where California forms its own region, there are 20 variables that affect choice of region.

8. The elasticity formulas for all three types are more complicated in the nested multinomial logit models (see Börsch-Supan 1987).

9. While prediction using the Box-Cox methodology is straightforward, inference (hypothesis testing) is problematic. For discussions of this topic, see Spitzer (1982) and Blackley, Follain, and Ondrich (1984).

Table 4B.1 Generalized Nested Logit Results for State and Region Choice by Foreign Investors: 1978-1987

	Model III	Model IV	Model V	Model VI
General State Variables:				
Log Relative Wage	0.179	0.114	0.181	-0.004
	(0.331)	(0.217)	(0.296)	(-0.008)
Employment Agglomeration	17.213	17.213	15.250	16.014
	(5.096)	(5.530)	(4.792)	(4.851)
Log Population	1.373	1.196	1.252	1.300
	(5.733)	(5.120)	(5.061)	(5.509)
Log Real Electric Bill x SIC 28	-0.630	-0.529	-0.613	-0.551
	(-1.683)	(-1.428)	(-1.631)	(-1.470)
Log Real Electric Bill x SIC 33	0.417	0.215	0.284	0.333
	(0.583)	(0.356)	(0.429)	(0.500)
Log Real Gas Bill x SIC 28	0.250	0.161	0.212	0.228
	(0.581)	(0.373)	(0.454)	(0.511)
Log Real Gas Bill x SIC 33	-0.614	-0.348	-0.440	-0.422
	(-0.795)	(-0.454)	(-0.528)	(-0.548)
Attractiveness for SIC 28	1.406	1.265	1.322	1.337
	(5.630)	(4.905)	(4.865)	(5.114)
Attractiveness for SIC 35	2.261	2.141	2.125	2.235
	(4.645)	(4.181)	(3.916)	(4.294)
Attractiveness for SIC 37	1.943	1.696	1.841	1.822
	(5.215)	(4.429)	(4.552)	(4.845)
State Fiscal Variables:				
Intergovernmental Aid	0.283	0.251	0.271	0.267
	(2.061)	(1.750)	(1.680)	(1.840)
Deficit	-0.401	-0.324	-0.323	-0.370
	(-2.455)	(-2.047)	(-1.814)	(-2.285)
Health Expenditures	0.275	0.164	0.179	0.224
	(1.478)	(0.836)	(0.854)	(1.180)
Highway Expenditures	-0.235	-0.222	-0.274	-0.218
	(-1.106)	(-0.965)	(-1.052)	(-0.969)
Primary and Secondary Education Expenditures	-0.224	-0.144	-0.210	-0.192
	(-1.200)	(-0.714)	(-0.975)	(-0.976)
Higher Education Expenditures	0.563	0.356	0.394	0.462
	(2.321)	(1.568)	(1.631)	(1.974)
Other Expenditures	0.090	0.025	0.041	0.082
	(0.563)	(0.155)	(0.230)	(0.503)

	Model III	Model IV	Model V	Model VI
Property Tax	-0.154	-0.170	-0.143	-0.153
	(-1.061)	(-1.120)	(-0.880)	(-1.024)
Sales Tax	-0.059	-0.067	-0.026	-0.061
	(-0.382)	(-0.398)	(-0.144)	(-0.372)
Individual Income Tax	0.021	0.018	0.058	0.029
	(0.143)	(0.114)	(0.347)	(0.193)
User Charges	-0.442	-0.304	-0.322	-0.372
	(-2.320)	(-1.643)	(-1.627)	(-2.029)
Corporate Tax	-0.440	-0.210	0.251	-0.354
	(-1.768)	(-0.771)	(-0.873)	(-1.291)
Corporate Tax x Unitary	-0.265	-0.101	0.029	-0.235
	(-0.979)	(-0.333)	(0.076)	(-0.808)
Other Taxes	-0.243	-0.210	-0.235	-0.215
	(-1.523)	(-1.303)	(-1.284)	(-1.310)
Regional Variables:				
Mountain Pacific				
Constant	0.115	-0.163	-0.187	-0.143
	(0.160)	(-0.149)	(-0.169)	(-0.139)
Europe	-1.250	-1.144	-1.155	-1.140
	(-2.706)	(-1.958)	(-1.917)	(-2.044)
Asia	-0.479	-0.977	-0.970	-0.975
	(-1.081)	(-1.688)	(-1.638)	(-1.763)
Log Real Transaction Value	0.063	0.257	0.260	0.257
	(0.731)	(2.258)	(2.247)	(2.213)
Dissimilarity Parameter	1.440	1.011	1.142	1.101
	(5.122)	(3.378)	(3.372)	(3.492)
West South Central				
Constant	-0.066	-0.247	0.046	-0.212
	(-0.070)	(-0.246)	(0.045)	(-0.216)
Europe	-0.263	-0.238	-0.261	-0.254
	(-0.449)	(-0.409)	(-0.434)	(-0.427)
Asia	-0.504	-0.535	-0.535	-0.531
	(-0.861)	(-0.901)	(-0.876)	(-0.893)
Log Real Transaction Value	0.197	0.202	0.202	0.202
	(1.845)	(1.912)	(1.869)	(1.918)
Dissimilarity Parameter	0.797	0.654	0.678	0.727
	(4.267)	(3.721)	(3.583)	(3.989)

	Model III	Model IV	Model V	Model VI
South				
Constant	2.456	2.382	2.558	2.337
	(3.474)	(3.328)	(3.374)	(3.443)
Europe	-0.453	-0.442	-0.445	-0.448
	(-1.134)	(-1.066)	(-1.084)	(-1.149)
Asia	-1.227	-1.237	-1.235	-1.228
	(-3.051)	(-2.989)	(-2.966)	(-3.093)
Log Real Transaction Value	-0.063	-0.062	-0.063	-0.061
	(-0.839)	(-0.834)	(-0.827)	(-0.804)
Dissimilarity Parameter	0.924	0.813	0.852	0.870
	(5.454)	(4.864)	(4.855)	(5.221)
Northeast				
Constant	2.582	1.872	--	2.503
	(3.352)	(2.182)		(3.352)
Europe	-1.030	-0.340	--	1.023
	(-2.559)	(-0.737)		(-2.632)
Asia	-2.055	-1.464	--	-2.045
	(-4.984)	(-3.061)		(-4.962)
Log Real Transaction Value	-0.292	-0.285	--	-0.293
	(-3.461)	(-3.019)		(-3.443)
Dissimilarity Parameter	1.677	1.632	--	1.600
	(5.121)	(4.171)		(4.893)
New England				
Constant	--	--	3.096	--
			(3.032)	
Europe	--	--	-0.445	--
			(-0.887)	
Asia	--	--	-1.994	--
			(-3.583)	
Log Real Transaction Value	--	--	-0.461	--
			(-3.967)	
Dissimilarity Parameter	--	--	1.993	--
			(3.535)	
Middle Atlantic				
Constant	--	--	2.870	--
			(3.212)	
Europe	--	--	-1.298	--
			(-3.033)	

	Model III	Model IV	Model V	Model VI
Asia	--	--	-2.052	--
			(-4.567)	
Log Real Transaction Value	--	--	-0.208	--
			(-2.187)	
Dissimilarity Parameter	--	--	1.349	--
			(2.962)	
California				
Constant	--	0.800	0.708	0.863
		(0.954)	(0.788)	(1.112)
Europe	--	-1.322	-1.325	-1.332
		(-2.377)	(-2.356)	(-2.520)
Asia	--	-0.174	-0.179	-0.178
		(-0.328)	(-0.334)	(-0.352)
Log Real Transaction Value	--	-0.064	-0.063	-0.063
		(-0.636)	(-0.609)	(-0.643)
New York				
Constant	--	4.202	--	--
		(4.814)		
Europe	--	-1.881	--	--
		(-4.218)		
Asia	--	-2.690	--	--
		(-5.531)		
Log Real Transaction Value	--	-0.316	--	--
		(-2.833)		
Midwest				
Dissimilarity Parameter	1.128	0.991	1.076	1.051
	(4.980)	(4.372)	(4.275)	(4.740)
Log-Likelihood	-3814.77	-3798.29	-3800.74	-3808.25

*t-statistics in parentheses.

5
The Potential Effect
of Changes in the Fiscal Policy
# of States on State Selection

In this chapter we present the results of three simulations aimed at discovering how specific changes in the fiscal policy of individual states would have affected the likelihood of their being selected by foreign direct investors over the period from 1978 to 1987. As we demonstrated in the preceding chapter, several state fiscal policies have considerable influence on whether a foreign firm decides to invest in that state. It is, therefore, valuable for states that desire to increase their share of the total of foreign direct investment to understand which specific components of their fiscal policy attract or impede foreign investment. Having identified these components in chapter 4, the simulation results presented below help to gauge the amount of foreign investment that is won or lost by the relative levels of these components.

The results from Model I in chapter 4 indicate that corporate taxes have a strong negative effect on the probability that a state is selected as a location for a new manufacturing plant, and that this effect is exacerbated, although insignificantly in a statistical sense, by the presence of a worldwide unitary tax structure in that state. On the other hand, using the results from Model I, we learn that individual income taxes have a small (insignificant) negative effect on state selection probability. If a given state eliminated its corporate tax and replaced it dollar for dollar with a higher individual income tax, the effect would be to increase its selection probability for each foreign investor (assuming of course that the initial level of corporate taxes was positive and not zero). This is the scenario for the first simulation, which we call Experiment I.

The second simulation, which we call Experiment II, uses the result from Model I that expenditures on higher education (per dollar of state personal income) have significant drawing power for new foreign manufacturing plants. Because this effect outweighs the effect of increasing the individual income tax, if the state were to finance a given increase in expenditures on higher education by raising its individual income tax, the net effect would be to increase the probability of a state's selection as a location for a new manufacturing plant. This is the scenario for the second simulation, in which expenditures on higher education (as a fraction of state personal income) are increased by 10 percent. This increase in expenditures is financed, dollar for dollar, by increasing individual income taxes.

The third simulation, which we call Experiment III, represents a combination of Experiments I and II. In this simulation, corporate taxes were eliminated for each state, and expenditures on higher education (as a fraction of state personal income) were increased by 10 percent. The combined increase in the deficit resulting from these fiscal changes was offset, dollar for dollar, by an increase in individual income taxes. Because Experiment III combines the effect of two fiscal policy changes that individually have a favorable effect on the state selection probability, the results from Experiment III must give the largest improvements in the state selection probabilities (except, of course, for those states which had no corporate taxes, and for which the results would be the same as in Experiment II).

Again, we emphasize that, within each simulation, the changes in the fiscal components for each state are made in such a way that the net effect of the changes on the overall deficit level is zero. Each simulation gives a result for the period from 1978 to 1987 for each state. The result for a given state assumes that only that state made a change in its fiscal structure and that all other states left their fiscal structures unchanged. In the simulations, therefore, we are abstracting from situations in which states might react to fiscal changes by other states to compete for FDI. Finally, we assume that the fiscal changes for each state in each simulation had been in place long enough before the beginning of the sample period so that all foreign firms who invested in the sample period knew about the altered fiscal status. Thus, we eliminate from our simulations considerations of expectations of fiscal policy changes.

The remainder of this chapter is divided into two sections. First, we discuss the way in which state selection probabilities can be expected to change as a result of the simulations. We then discuss the theoretical underpinnings for the results and draw some conclusions.

Simulation Details and Presentation

This section has two goals. The first goal is to describe the manner in which state selection probabilities are likely to change as a result of the fiscal policy changes within the simulation. The second goal is to describe how the simulation results are presented in the next section.

Let us move towards the first goal by asking whether certain simulation results are inherent in the design or estimation of the model. The answer is no. Because we use the multinomial logit model, the state selection probabilities are a nonlinear function of the deterministic profit components (and therefore of the covariates which comprise them). Given the nonlinearity of the relationship, the magnitude of the effect of a change in a fiscal policy variable depends on its interaction with other covariates in the model. Thus, the simulations do not yield results that can be anticipated from the magnitude of the particular covariate undergoing the policy change. Put differently, the magnitude of the change is entirely an empirical question.

Having said this, we examine certain situations that may help us gain a better understanding of the simulation results. The first point to remember here is that in the model specifications the actual dollar levels in the various tax and expenditure categories do not enter the deterministic component of the stochastic profit function, which is positively related to the selection probability for that state. Thus, the fact that the actual dollar levels in the tax and expenditure categories are higher for New York than for Montana is not a reason that the selection probabilities for New York will be higher (or for that matter, lower) than the selection probabilities for Montana. All fiscal variables enter the deterministic components of stochastic profit functions as a fraction of state personal income.   The fiscal structure of one state is more attractive to foreign investors than the fiscal structure of a second state only insofar as the first state generally has the higher values as a fraction of state personal income in the more favorable fiscal categories. Similarly, the selection probability of one state will change more than the selection probability of a second state as a result of a simulation, all else equal, to the extent that the simulation implies a greater shift of these fractions to the more favorable fiscal categories for the first state.

The second situation which we wish to examine can best be addressed by asking the following question. Will states with higher or with lower initial selection probabilities exhibit the greatest percentage changes in these probabilities in response to a given fiscal policy change (expressed as a fraction of state personal income)? If, as a result of a simulated policy change, two states had the same change in deterministic profit levels, the state with the smaller initial selection probability will have the larger percentage change in the state selection probability.

While we show this result formally below, a policy change need not result in the same change in the deterministic profit levels in any two states. Thus, whether states with lower selection probabilities have a greater percentage change in their selection probabilities is in part an empirical question. Nonetheless, this result will help explain why some smaller states realize larger percentage changes in their selection probabilities under some of the simulations.

To begin our formal derivation of the above results, let us define π_{ds} to be the deterministic profit level or a given firm in state s. Then the firm's selection probability for state i is given by

$$P(i) = \exp[\pi_{di}] / \sum_s \exp[\pi_{ds}] , \qquad (5.1)$$

where the summation in the denominator is over all states s. A simple calculation gives the derivative of $P(i)$ with respect to π_{di} as

$$d\,P(i) / d\pi_{di} = P(i)(1 - P(i)) . \qquad (5.2)$$

The right-hand-side of equation (5.2) reaches a maximum at

$$P(i) = 0.5 . \qquad (5.3)$$

Because the highest empirical state selection probability is only slightly greater than 0.1 (in the case of California), we can safely assume that the greatest increase in the level of the state selection probabilities per unit change in the deterministic profit level occurs for those states with the highest initial selection probabilities. However, the answer to our question is altered when we examine situations that produce the greatest percentage changes in the state selection probabilities.

For example, rearranging equation (5.2) by dividing both sides by $P(i)$, we obtain

$$(dP(i) / d\pi_{ds}) / (P(i) = (1 - P(i)) , \qquad (5.4)$$

which says that the percentage change in the state selection probability is greater per unit change in the state's deterministic profit level, the smaller the initial selection probability.

We turn now to a description of the statistics presented in the simulation results in the next section. In each of the three simulations, each of the 1,184 firms in our estimation sample will have a state selection probability for each state. Needless to say, it is not feasible to present information on each firm in all states. We present the expectation (expected value) of the number of firms that chose to locate in the given state under each fiscal scenario. This expectation is calculated as the state's average selection probability (or the average probability over the 1,184 firms evaluated at relevant values of the covariates using parameter estimates from the Model I standard multinomial logit) multiplied by 1,184, the number of firms in the sample. For each state in each simulation, the old expectation given is the expectation evaluated at the actual (historical) values of the covariates. A new expectation can then be calculated which is the expectation evaluated at the new covariate values applicable to the specific simulation. The percentage change figure that we compute is the difference between the new expectation and the old expectation divided by the old expectation.

Simulation Results

The results of the simulations are reviewed in detail below. As the empirical results reported in the previous chapter imply, there is significant variation in the responsiveness of FDI location to different fiscal variables. There is also large variation in the location response among states to a given fiscal stimulus.

Corporate Tax Elimination

The first simulation examines the effect on a state's expected number of new foreign plants if that state and only that state eliminates its corporate income tax and raises the lost revenue through its individual income tax. The results refer in particular to the percentage increase in the new plants attracted to a state during the entire 1978 to 1987 period and in each of two years—1979 and 1987. The percentage changes are reported in table 5.1 along with the baseline or initial values of new foreign plants for each state. In the text, we discuss the results for the entire period only. The experiment produces relatively high percentage changes in the number of foreign plants when one state undergoes the policy change. While the percentage changes imply very different numbers of plants in states due to different baseline values in each state, the percentage changes appear the best indicator of the impact of the policy change from the point of view of the individual state.

The percentage change in the number of new plants in each state for the entire 1978 to 1987 period under Experiment I is illustrated in figure 5.1, where the percentage change results are grouped by quartile. The elimination of the corporate income tax has powerful effects in a substantial number of states, if they act alone. The other side of this issue is that the simultaneous increase in the individual income tax does not substantially reduce the number of foreign plants, or at least the net effect of the combined corporate/individual income tax policy is quite large. The elimination of a state's corporate income tax would have the largest impact (fourth quartile) for the States of Massachusetts, California, New Hampshire, Michigan, and North Dakota, Montana, Oregon, Minnesota, Illinois, Connecticut, Delaware, and Idaho. Seven of these states have relatively high corporate tax rates. However, the smaller population states among them have corporate tax burdens around the median value for states. Of course, the policy has no impact in states without a corporate income tax.

There are two major caveats to this conclusion. States will rarely act alone. A state that eliminates its corporate income tax will likely have imitators. Other states will begin to compete by following the same fiscal strategy, and the first-mover advantages will begin to dissipate as more states follow the leader. Thus, the estimates reported here over-

Table 5.1 Experiment I
Percentage Change in Expected Number of Foreign
Manufacturing Plants Induced by Eliminating the State
Corporate Tax Financed by Higher Individual Income Taxes,
1978 through 1987, 1979 Only, and 1987 Only

State	Overall Old expectation	Overall Percent change	1979 Old expectation	1979 Percent change	1987 Old expectation	1987 Percent change
Alabama	41.207	18.70	7.204	17.89	5.863	15.80
Arizona	9.344	23.16	2.033	20.88	0.638	21.25
Arkansas	10.620	24.74	1.765	28.18	1.045	22.05
California	120.000	67.35	10.858	84.41	17.232	75.95
Colorado	13.149	22.28	2.573	35.18	1.355	11.93
Connecticut	27.096	38.70	4.442	35.69	2.231	56.84
Delaware	11.841	37.28	3.053	49.21	0.586	58.99
Florida	53.136	16.88	8.383	18.62	4.403	15.68
Georgia	49.620	25.11	8.166	27.96	4.090	25.81
Idaho	3.808	36.94	0.513	48.63	0.699	34.27
Illinois	44.079	38.72	5.706	34.98	5.677	37.48
Indiana	26.434	13.43	4.116	13.05	4.168	14.98
Iowa	6.097	21.83	0.680	26.06	1.560	19.35
Kansas	4.703	27.08	0.765	35.72	0.743	18.90
Kentucky	25.310	27.62	2.445	32.41	3.149	31.27
Louisiana	10.446	31.28	2.657	36.48	2.322	18.80
Maine	5.747	21.58	0.868	26.47	0.633	21.41
Maryland	23.883	16.21	3.213	18.02	3.796	16.25
Massachusetts	37.595	70.58	5.364	86.64	3.297	63.02
Michigan	39.286	58.47	4.553	64.91	5.643	64.25
Minnesota	6.180	40.49	1.037	56.89	0.887	34.60
Mississippi	21.890	19.14	3.843	18.18	2.544	19.34
Missouri	18.477	13.49	2.551	15.46	2.382	15.79
Montana	1.006	49.63	0.203	51.35	0.110	29.24
Nebraska	3.243	16.53	0.500	18.61	0.598	15.22
Nevada	1.152	0.00	0.234	0.00	0.187	0.00
New Hampshire	3.466	60.53	0.486	80.89	0.514	45.46
New Jersey	41.269	32.07	5.668	28.80	4.552	35.93
New Mexico	2.415	22.98	0.589	22.17	0.148	30.24

State	Overall Old expectation	Overall Percent change	1979 Old expectation	1979 Percent change	1987 Old expectation	1987 Percent change
New York	78.393	32.59	16.614	3 4.29	7.168	33.82
North Carolina	78.102	28.88	8.826	30.42	9.475	33.14
North Dakota	0.540	50.25	0.052	47.79	0.093	33.24
Ohio	43.734	19.04	5.447	26.17	7.995	1 3.59
Oklahoma	9.732	16.39	1.765	19.49	0.885	10.07
Oregon	8.741	41.01	1.161	67.06	1.895	18.29
Pennsylvania	45.490	33.73	6.465	43.05	4.486	28.66
Rhode Island	6.085	29.54	1.224	38.32	0.500	30.63
South Carolina	38.173	27.89	6.284	34.38	3.711	23.51
South Dakota	1.035	5.88	0.198	2.51	0.100	13.92
Tennessee	39.306	25.01	4.902	29.02	4.485	24.17
Texas	81.201	0.00	13.031	0.00	7.795	0.00
Utah	7.225	22.14	0.997	25.83	1.398	15.87
Vermont	4.857	26.55	0.769	33.10	0.236	26.25
Virginia	39.576	16.53	4.746	21.46	4.879	16.12
Washington	18.260	0.00	2.993	0.00	3.981	0.00
West Virginia	4.957	15.62	0.777	9.01	0.464	22.55
Wisconsin	15.192	35.75	2.010	43.46	1.375	36.69
Wyoming	0.898	0.00	0.268	0.00	0.027	0.00

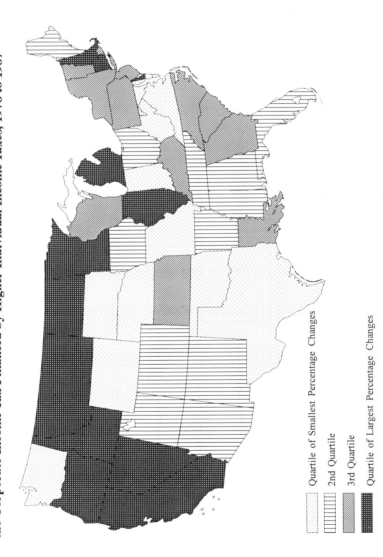

Figure 5.1 Experiment I
Percentage Change in the Expected Number of Foreign Manufacturing Plants Induced by Eliminating the Corporate Income Tax Financed by Higher Individual Income Taxes, 1978 to 1987

Quartile of Smallest Percentage Changes

2nd Quartile

3rd Quartile

Quartile of Largest Percentage Changes

state what would happen if many or all states eliminated their corporate income tax. In addition, the model does not capture any feedback effects when the state raises its individual income tax to compensate for the revenue lost by elimination of the corporate tax. For example, population outmigration might result when individual income taxes are increased in a state. That, in turn, could affect the attractiveness of a state to foreign investors, especially if skilled workers migrate in significant numbers.

One cannot, therefore, take the simulation results too literally. We draw the conclusion that corporate income taxes are powerful deterrents to foreign firms. High corporate taxes reduce the probability of attracting a foreign firm. Nonetheless, other advantages in the state can offset an unfavorable corporate income tax position. For example, California has attracted significant foreign investment, despite having a worldwide unitary tax (although it was eliminated in 1988) and a relatively high effective corporate tax rate.

Increasing Higher Education Expenditures

We ran another simulation in which higher education expenditures are increased 10 percent in a particular state and the extra expenditures are financed through higher individual income taxes. The higher education policy simulation is run very similarly to the corporate income tax policy simulation, as described above. It was run for the overall 1978 to 1987 period and then for each of two years, 1979 and 1987. In addition, the simulation assumes that a state increases its higher education expenditures and finances it with higher individual income taxes with no corresponding action in other states. The results are reported in table 5.2, and the results are illustrated in figure 5.2 by quartile of percentage changes.

The first observation is that the percentage changes for Experiment II are not large relative to those for the corporate income tax. This is explained in part by the fact that the change in higher education expenditures only requires only about one-half of the increase in individual income taxes compared to what the elimination of the corporate income tax rate requires. Even adjusting for the magnitude of the policy change, however, the increase in higher education expenditures in

Table 5.2 Experiment II
Percentage Change in the Expected Number of Foreign Manufacturing Plants Induced by Increasing State Higher Education Expenditures Financed by Higher Individual Income Taxes, 1978 through 1987, 1979 Only, and 1987 Only

State	Overall Old expectation	Overall Percent change	1979 Old expectation	1979 Percent change	1987 Old expectation	1987 Percent change
Alabama	41.207	12.50	7.204	12.19	5.863	12.44
Arizona	9.344	14.71	2.033	14.36	0.638	14.66
Arkansas	10.620	9.46	1.765	8.88	1.045	10.64
California	120.000	8.45	10.858	7.841	7.232	8.59
Colorado	13.149	11.54	2.573	12.90	1.355	11.22
Connecticut	27.096	4.25	4.442	4.30	2.231	4.23
Delaware	11.841	14.51	3.053	13. 52	0.586	14.91
Florida	53.136	6.19	8.383	6.64	4.403	4.97
Georgia	49.620	8.19	8.166	8.56	4.090	7.69
Idaho	3.808	12.35	0.513	10.07	0.699	14.79
Illinois	4.079	7 .23	5.706	6.45	5.677	8.00
Indiana	26.434	10.54	4.116	9.36	4.168	12.15
Iowa	6.097	14.60	0.680	12.67	1.560	16.43
Kansas	4.703	11.95	0.765	12.16	0.743	12.31
Kentucky	25.310	10.64	2.445	11.30	3.149	10.91
Louisiana	10.446	10.18	2.657	9.65	2.322	10.79
Maine	5.747	8.35	0.868	7.82	0.633	8.78
Maryland	23.883	8.70	3.213	9.3 1	3.796	8.52
Massachusetts	37.595	4.36	5.364	4.33	3.297	5.30
Michigan	39.286	10.85	4553	10.11	5.643	11.77
Minnesota	6.180	10.87	1.037	10.01	0.887	13.02
Mississippi	21.890	13.83	3.843	13.84	2.544	13.27
Missouri	18.477	7.38	2.551	6.73	2.382	9.05
Montana	1.006	10.11	0.203	9.91	0.110	11.34
Nebraska	3.243	12.30	0.500	12.07	0.598	13.59
Nevada	1.152	7.12	0.234	6.86	0.187	7.25
New Hampshire	3.466	6 .85	0.486	7.68	0.514	5.88
New Jersey	41.269	5.04	5.668	5.03	4.552	5.69
New Mexico	2.415	16.68	0.589	16.56	0.148	15.64

State	Overall		1979		1987	
	Old expectation	Percent change	Old expectation	Percent change	Old expectation	Percent change
New York	78.393	6.26	16.614	6.11	7.168	6.66
North Carolina	78.102	12.13	8.826	12.14	9.475	12.51
North Dakota	0.540	17.20	0.052	13.41	0.093	19.35
Ohio	43.734	8.41	5.447	7.70	7.995	9.03
Oklahoma	9.732	11.44	1.765	10.81	0.885	11.34
Oregon	8.741	12.93	1.161	11.81	1.895	13.29
Pennsylvania	45.490	4.41	6.465	4.29	4.486	4.86
Rhode Island	6.085	8.86	1.224	9.14	0.500	7.81
South Carolina	38.173	12.17	6.284	12.72	3.711	13.24
South Dakota	1.035	11.77	0.198	13.80	0.100	11.60
Tennessee	39.306	9.01	4.902	8.73	4.485	9.43
Texas	81.201	9.47	13.031	8.62	7.795	10.42
Utah	7.225	19.00	0.997	18.07	1.398	20.72
Vermont	4.857	14.96	0.769	15.57	0.236	14.15
Virginia	39.576	9.16	4.746	9.55	4.879	9.58
Washington	18.260	11.48	2.993	11.78	3.981	11.21
West Virginia	4.957	10.14	0.777	11.09	0.464	10.38
Wisconsin	15.192	13.98	2.010	13.16	1.375	13.84
Wyoming	0.898	14.62	0.268	12.61	0.027	19.88

Figure 5.2 Experiment II
Percentage Change in the Expected Number of Foreign Manufacturing Plants Induced by Increasing
Higher Education Expenditures Financed by Higher Individual Income Taxes, 1978 to 1987

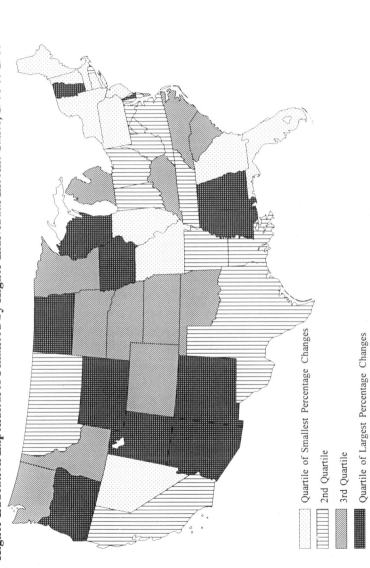

Quartile of Smallest Percentage Changes

2nd Quartile

3rd Quartile

Quartile of Largest Percentage Changes

larger states has smaller effects relative to the elimination of the corporate income tax.

The states that have the largest percentage changes in new foreign manufacturing plants as a result of changing their higher education expenditures are low population states that spend a larger proportion of their income to support public higher education. The states with the largest effects, for example, include Utah, North Dakota, New Mexico, Vermont, Arizona, Wyoming, Iowa, and Delaware. While the two caveats that apply to the corporate income tax apply in this case, it is the smaller states for which the higher education strategy would appear to pay off the most.

Elimination of Corporate Income Tax and More for Higher Education

We have also performed a simulation in which we eliminate the corporate income tax and increase higher education expenditures by 10 percent, financing that package with higher individual income taxes. The results of the simulation reflect the effect for an individual state when it alone enacts the fiscal policy change. As such, the caveats mentioned above apply here as well.

In effect, the combined policies represent almost a linear combination of the two separate simulations reported above. The results of the combined simulation are reported in table 5.3 and are illustrated in figure 5.3. The corporate income tax effect is the dominant of the two policies and the rank order of the states from adopting the combined policy changes are not much different from the rankings reported for the simulation of the corporate tax elimination policy.

Other Policy Levers

Based on our results, states have relatively few policy levers to attract foreign investment. For example, states have almost no direct control over their agglomeration economies and their population (or market) size that prove to be very dominant factors governing the location choices of foreign manufacturers. Moreover, in our analysis, fiscal variables, except for the corporate income tax and higher education

Table 5.3 Percentage Change in the Expected Number of Foreign Manufacturing Plants Induced by Increasing State Higher Education Expenditures and Eliminating the State Corporate Tax Financed by Higher Individual Income Taxes, 1978 through 1987, 1979 Only, and 1987 Only

State	Overall Old expectation	Overall Percent change	1979 Old expectation	1979 Percent change	1987 Old expectation	1987 Percent change
Alabama	41.207	33.40	7.204	32.11	5.863	30.06
Arizona	9.344	41.22	2.033	38.17	0.638	39.00
Arkansas	10.620	36.49	1.765	39.52	1.045	35.01
California	120. 000	79.82	10.858	97.50	7.232	88.91
Colorado	13.149	36.40	2.573	52.48	1.355	24.46
Connecticut	27.096	44.46	4.442	41.40	2.231	63.33
Delaware	11.841	56.79	3.053	68.71	0.586	82.47
Florida	53.136	24.05	8.383	26.42	4.403	21.40
Georgia	49.620	35.22	8.166	38.73	4.090	35.39
Idaho	3.808	53.76	0.513	63.56	0.699	54.08
Illinois	4.079	48.56	5.706	43.56	5.677	48.27
Indiana	26.434	25.33	4.116	23.58	4.168	28.87
Iowa	6.097	39.55	0.680	42.00	1.560	38.90
Kansas	4.703	42.23	0.765	52.19	0.743	33.51
Kentucky	25.310	41.05	2.445	47.25	3.149	45.42
Louisiana	10.446	44.52	2.657	49.52	2.322	31.56
Maine	5.747	31.70	0.868	36.34	0.633	32.05
Maryland	23.883	26.28	3.213	28.96	3.796	26.10
Massachusetts	37.595	77.76	5.364	94.44	3.297	71.47
Michigan	39.286	75.01	4553	81.08	5.643	82.66
Minnesota	6.180	55.67	1.037	72.53	0.887	52.08
Mississippi	21.890	35.53	3.843	34.46	2.544	35.10
Missouri	18.477	21.85	2.551	23.20	2.382	26.23
Montana	1.006	64.65	0.203	66.33	0.110	· 43.90
Nebraska	3.243	30.84	0.500	32.71	0.598	30.86
Nevada	1.152	7.12	0.234	6.86	0.187	7.25
New Hampshire	3.466	71.58	0.486	94.74	0.514	53.99
New Jersey	41.269	38.60	5.668	35.18	4.552	43.48
New Mexico	2.415	43.46	0.589	42.37	0.148	50.60

State	Overall		1979		1987	
	Old expectation	Percent change	Old expectation	Percent change	Old expectation	Percent change
New York	78.393	40.62	16.614	42.12	7.168	42.50
North Carolina	78.102	44.12	8.826	45.92	9.475	49.30
North Dakota	0.540	76.11	0.052	67.60	0.093	59.01
Ohio	43.734	28.90	5.447	35.75	7.995	23.69
Oklahoma	9.732	26.67	1.765	32.38	0.885	22.55
Oregon	8.741	59.10	1.161	86.66	1.895	33.96
Pennsylvania	45.490	39.51	6.465	49.06	4.486	34.83
Rhode Island	6.085	40.99	1.224	50.91	0.500	40.81
South Carolina	38.173	43.26	6.284	51.17	3.711	39.73
South Dakota	1.035	18.30	0.198	16.66	0.100	27.14
Tennessee	39.306	36.17	4.902	40.18	4.485	35.77
Texas	81.201	9.47	13.031	8.62	7.795	10.42
Utah	7.225	45.26	0.997	48.51	1.398	39.83
Vermont	4.857	45.44	0.769	53.78	0.236	44.09
Virginia	39.576	27.14	4.74 6	32.98	4.879	27.17
Washington	18.260	11.48	2.993	11.78	3.981	11.21
West Virginia	4.957	27.36	0.777	21.09	0.464	35.26
Wisconsin	15.192	54.60	2.010	62.21	1.37 5	55.52
Wyoming	0.898	14.62	0.268	12.61	0.027	19.88

Figure 5.3 Experiment III
Percentage Change in the Expected Number of Foreign Manufacturing Plants Induced by Increasing Higher Education Expenditures and Eliminating the Corporate Income Tax Financed by Higher Individual Income Taxes, 1978 to 1987

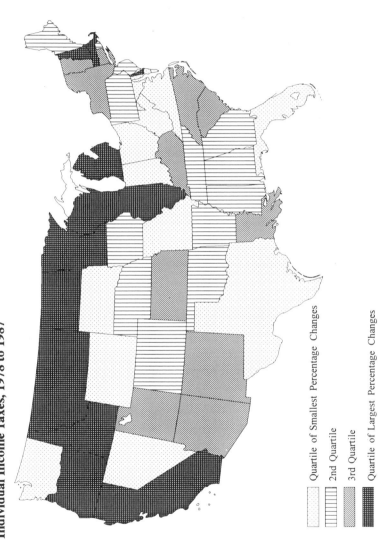

Quartile of Smallest Percentage Changes

2nd Quartile

3rd Quartile

Quartile of Largest Percentage Changes

expenditures, have limited impacts on foreign investors location decisions.

States typically use a number of economic development strategies and incentives in attempts to attract firms, such as explicit tax incentive packages, worker training allowances and programs, and subsidized interest loans (Bartik 1991). While the magnitude of the effects of these programs on location is largely unknown, states use them regularly to attract major companies to their state. Our results do indicate that such programs offering corporate income tax relief may affect the location of foreign firms, but that generally speaking states do not have a wide array of policy handles available to attract foreign firms. States with agglomeration in that industry or a sizable population in or near the state will likely remain attractive locations for foreign manufacturing plants.

6
Conclusions
and
Policy Implications

The conclusions that emerge from our investigation of foreign direct investment are put together here with those of other researchers to formulate what we believe is a coherent body of information about FDI in the United States during the 1978 to 1987 period. While using results garnered from analysis of a decade of data to characterize foreign direct investment can be somewhat risky, we believe that the consistency of many of our results with the findings of other researchers lends credibility to the conclusions we draw. In this chapter, we focus on our major results and policy conclusions. We also focus, where appropriate, on the facts that state and local policymakers should consider when they bid to attract foreign direct investors.

We reiterate that most of the total (portfolio and direct) foreign investment in the United States is done by four countries: United Kingdom, Japan, the Netherlands, and Canada, listed in order of their total assets in the United States. These four countries dominate in each of the portfolio and foreign direct investment categories of investment. However, during the 1980s Japan had the highest rate of growth of assets in the United States.

The United States still maintains a surplus (outward minus inward) position in FDI, but it has decreased in recent years with inward investment flows dominating outward flows. By contrast the United States has had a negative position in its portfolio investment since 1985.

Benefits and Costs of FDI: Restrictions on Capital Inflows

We have weighed several arguments about the benefits and potential costs of FDI in the United States. On balance, we believe that it has helped to stabilize our economy, providing jobs for 9.3 percent of the U.S. manufacturing workforce. Moreover, the new foreign manufacturing plants built in the United States between 1978 and 1987 were overwhelmingly concentrated in four major industry groups: Chemicals and Allied Products, Industrial Machinery and Equipment, Electronic and Other Electric Equipment, and Transportation Equipment. In 1992, for example, workers in two of the major industry groups, Chemicals and Allied Products and Transportation Equipment, typically earned more than 20 percent per hour more than the average worker in manufacturing. Workers in the Industrial Machinery and Equipment major group earned 6 percent more than the average in manufacturing, while workers in the Electronic and Other Electric Equipment major group earned 6 percent less per hour than the average in manufacturing. Despite the earnings in the last category, we conclude that FDI in manufacturing creates largely well-paying jobs.

We acknowledge, however, that continued dominance of worldwide investment by investors other than Americans would, over time, make us relatively less well off as a people. Thus, we share the concern that many advocates for increased worldwide investment by Americans have expressed.

Nonetheless, the present debate on U.S. trade policy includes arguments for restricting capital inflows to the United States for purposes of gaining strategic advantage in negotiations that would allow American producers access to some foreign markets. Such a policy, if adopted, would put existing state efforts to recruit new plants at odds with federal policy. States have every incentive to keep recruiting foreign investors, because the advantages of attracting foreign plants to any particular state's citizens are likely to mask the nationwide economic costs of increased foreign investment when all states pursue their narrow interests and continue efforts to attract foreign investors.

We caution, however, against restricting states' activities to attract foreign investment. We believe that for a variety of reasons, such restrictions would do more harm than good, even in the longer term. Our rationale, simply put, is that investment decisions are increasingly made in a global economy. U.S. investors may find investments in Mexico, Canada, and elsewhere relatively more rewarding in the near future than they have in the past. In addition, economic income from investment will be determined from ownership of global capital rather than of domestic capital only. Thus, restricting foreign investment in the United States may set up uneconomic incentives for U.S. capitalists to invest here rather than abroad and induce misallocation of America's capital and lower its long-term income growth. Moreover, the creation of American jobs by foreign firms speeds the transfer of technology and managerial knowledge to this country.

Aside from the economic arguments, restrictions on FDI appear difficult to implement, because states engage in direct recruitment efforts. To control investment, states might have to submit proposals for FDI to a federal review board, where appropriate controls could be imposed. A lengthy review process would add to the costs of FDI and, depending on whether each state was given a particular number of FDI projects, could induce inefficient location patterns.

For all of these reasons, we conclude that the imposition of restrictions on FDI is not good policy. Policies undertaken to increase domestic saving and, in turn, investment here and abroad will yield better long-term income growth in the United States and avoid inefficiencies associated with capital inflow restrictions.

Where Should States Seek FDI?

We have focused, in this monograph, on new manufacturing plants built in the United States between 1978 and 1987. The home countries of investors building new foreign manufacturing plants in the United States are somewhat different from the above list of major investors, however. In order of their importance, Japan, Germany, the United Kingdom, and Canada built most of the new manufacturing plants in the United States during the 1978 to 1987 period, with Japan and Germany responsible for over one-half of the new plants in our data. States searching for investors might be tempted to begin with these countries as the potential sources of direct investment. However, with the recent recombination of West and East Germany, German investment in the 1990s may be more concentrated in Germany than in the United States. At this time, Japanese direct investment in the United States has also dampened. Thus, states should seek investors with new ideas and efficient production techniques in the state's major industries. Countries that have high productivity will likely generate significant domestic saving that can be invested abroad. These countries can also reap the first-mover advantages associated with early penetration into a new country or market. Also, if the United States imposes trade restrictions in certain goods, FDI or production in the United States represents an opportunity to circumvent those restrictions. Thus, federal trade restrictions create FDI opportunities for states.

While new foreign plants were constructed in 19 of the 20 major manufacturing industry groups, plants were primarily built, as mentioned above, in four major industry groups: Chemicals and Allied Products, Industrial Machinery and Equipment, Electronic and Other Electric Equipment, and Transportation Equipment, listed in order of the number of plants built. Investors from Germany, Japan, the United Kingdom, and Canada also tended to dominate as the major builders of new plants in these four major groups. However, investors from Switzerland and France were major new plant builders in several of the four major groups.

The location of new plants was concentrated in relatively few states. Staying with the four major industry groups cited above, Texas, North Carolina, and New Jersey captured a major share of the new foreign plants in Chemicals and Allied Products, while California and Georgia captured a major share of the new plant investment in Electronic and Electrical Equipment. New plants in the Industrial Machinery and Equipment major group tended to locate in North Carolina, California, Connecticut, and Georgia. Ohio, Michigan, Tennessee, California, and Illinois captured a major share of the new plants in the Transportation Equipment major group.

When all industries and all home investor countries are considered, California, Georgia, Illinois, New York, North Carolina, Texas, and Tennessee each received 50 or more new foreign plants during the 1978 to 1987 period. The locations of most of the rest of the new plants were concentrated in the eastern half of the United States.

What Attracts FDI to States?

FDI is driven by market size, agglomeration economies, and, to a lesser extent, cost and fiscal factors. In what follows, we review the major findings of the study, and, where appropriate, compare them to those in the recent literature on FDI location.

Markets

First, we do not find that per capita income and the growth of per capita income in a state are important variables for attracting foreign investors. While other authors have found that per capita income is significant in determining state location choice, their conclusions are generally based on cross-sectional data rather than a pooled cross-section time-series sample. Still, our results suggest that regional markets are not significant variables in the determination of new plant locations, and that requires further explanation.

Two explanations for the above result are possible. First, drawing on the results in a separate literature on the determinants of aggregate-investment flows to the United States, we suggest that the sizable market in the United States as well as international trade barriers that prevent certain goods from entering the United States determine the willingness of investors to build new manufacturing plants somewhere within the United States. One might conclude that most of the new plants are producing for the U.S. market in general and, once the decision to locate in the United States is made, the per capita income of a particular state has little, if any, influence on the investor's decision to locate a new manufacturing plant in that state. Production for a U.S. market may be especially the case for the plants in the four major industry groups that dominate the sample.

An alternative explanation is that the population size of the state, which has a significant coefficient and relatively large elasticity for FDI location, has measured market potential in the model rather than the per capita income level or growth variables. Thus, population size represents regional market potential as well as an available workforce.

Wages

We do not find that real wages in a state influence the location of a new foreign plant in a significant way. We are somewhat surprised by that result. We reason that investors might regard U.S. wages as high relative to the rest of the world and, in the case of the United States, wages do not play a significant role in decisions of foreign investors to locate here. Carried one step further, wage variation within the United States is not of sufficient consequence to foreign investors to influence their state location choices. Added to our evidence is that other researchers have not uniformly found that wages influence FDI location decisions among states or within states. For example, one researcher (Woodward 1992), who has examined the state as well as the county locations of Japanese investments, does not find that wages are a significant determinant of the state location or the county location choice within the state. Other variables apparently drive the location choices of foreign plants. For example, the set of states with the specified desirable characteristics may not have significant variation in wage rates among them. The caveat is that we and others are unable to account completely for labor productivity differences across states, and that could bias the results on the wage variable.

Agglomeration

Agglomeration economies measured here as a high concentration of employment in the major industry group within a state have proved a powerful locational determinant for foreign manufacturing plants. So powerful are the agglomeration effects in three industries that in the estimation we have had to take special account of the attraction of Chemicals and Allied Products to Alabama, Delaware, Louisiana, New Jersey, and Texas, of Industrial Machinery and Equipment to Connecticut, and of Transportation Equipment to Kentucky, Michigan, and Ohio.

The findings about agglomeration economies are interesting and need interpretation. To some extent, the finding implies that FDI in manufacturing plants typically occurs in the traditional areas of manufacturing strength in a state. However, a large share of the FDI in manufacturing plants has located in 10 relatively highly populated states. Thus, the relative concentration of the industry group in question as well as the fact that the industry group has a relatively large presence in a relatively large state economy, measured by number of employees or capital investment, makes a state attractive as a location for a foreign manufacturing state. Access to the skilled labor pool in that industry, proximity to similar firms or to networks of intermediate input suppliers, and availability of information about market trends and technological change in the industry represent the major advantages conferred by agglomeration. However, a less populated state, such as Delaware or Wyoming, for example, might have a relative agglomeration in a major group and still not attract FDI. Those states may not have enough of any industry to reap the substantial gains that arise from the absolute size of an industry's presence.

Another implication of the results for the agglomeration economies variable concerns the fact that foreign investors compete with firms in the state's traditional major industry group. At the national level, Ray (1989) argues that FDI may displace traditional domestic industries, and there is some question as to whether such foreign investment should be encouraged. However, from an individual state's vantage point, the new foreign manufacturing plant will probably locate somewhere within the United States (perhaps in a neighboring state) and compete with the domestic producers located in the state in question anyway. Thus, not inviting the new plant to a particular state will not substantially reduce the competition its existing firms face in the global or even the national economy. A state would be wise to capitalize on its comparative advantage in a particular industry group and recruit similar types of firms to build plants in the state.

Fiscal Effects

We have also done a significant amount of work modeling the fiscal effects of state and local expenditures and taxes on location choice. Taxation of foreign corporations is an especially complicated area, because whether taxes in the host country matter at all depends on home country tax policy toward foreign investment, as well as a large number of factors that underlie the effective tax rate of the foreign plant. We have employed Helms (1985) budget constraint in our model, modified by the state's stance on taxation of multinational firms. Helms' method requires choosing a numeraire and interpreting the coefficients relative to the numeraire. Following Helms, we have chosen welfare spending as the numeraire and find that states with a higher deficit or higher user charges to finance higher welfare spending deterred the location of new foreign plants. Lower spending on higher education to finance welfare expenditure is also a deterrent to location of new foreign plants. States with higher corporate income taxes will deter new foreign plants from locating within them.

The results for the corporate income tax are so strong that we have devised simulations to explore the effect on the probability of attracting more foreign plants if in any single state the corporate income tax were eliminated and the revenues were raised using the state personal income tax instead. The simulations suggest that the shift away from the corporate income tax would have a very strong positive effect on the number of foreign plants locating within a state. We emphasize, however, that tax policy changes of this magnitude typically have a large number of other implications that affect firm and household decisions about locating within the state. Our simulations could not take into account many of the other implications of eliminating the corporate income tax. Our results are, therefore, suggestive of the strong influence that corporate income taxes have on the location of foreign plants. Put another way, reducing corporate taxes would make the state more attractive to foreign manufacturing plants, but eliminating the corporate income tax would surely have behavioral repercussions that could dampen the strong effect that we report in the simulations.

The magnitude of our results for the corporate income tax effect differs substantially from the weak role that other researchers find. We attribute the difference to our more careful modeling of the state and local budget. Most other research partially models state and local taxes, and virtually ignores the expenditure side of the fiscal picture. Apparently, the improved modeling of the fiscal sector leads to our more precise results.

Another dimension of tax policy is unitary taxation. During certain times in the 10-year analysis period, as many as 11 states used a worldwide unitary definition of the income of foreign corporations. A tax, such as worldwide unitary, that is specifically directed at FDI might be expected to deter FDI substantially. Nonetheless, we do not find, as other researchers have, that the use of worldwide unitary taxation had a significant effect on the locations of new foreign plants. We attribute our finding to using a longer period of analysis and the fact that many states were phasing out worldwide unitary taxation during the time period of our analysis. For example, a substantial number of new manufacturing plants located in California during the 1978 to 1987 period, and California operated a worldwide unitary tax system during that period. However, in 1988 California eliminated its worldwide unitary tax and moved to a water's edge unitary definition.[1] Foreign investors probably anticipated its elimination and thus the unitary tax was not a deterrent to location in California during a significant portion of our analysis period. In Florida, the worldwide unitary tax was abolished after one year. Similar stories can be told in other states.

To close, we believe that FDI has significant employment effects in states. States seeking to attract such investment might look beyond the traditional four countries, because Germany and Japan may not now have the substantial pools of domestic saving to invest here. States will find opportunities for FDI from countries with high productivity which has typically produced high savings rates. These countries may be looking for first-mover advantages in investing abroad or for avoidance of tariff or other trade barriers that may have been imposed on the importation of their products. Those situations seem to produce high potential for FDI.

Furthermore, states can make themselves more attractive to FDI by reducing corporate income taxes and maintaining a high-quality system of higher education. However, populous states with large concentrations of the FDI industry in question have received most of the FDI in manufacturing. We expect size and agglomeration will continue to play a major role in state-level FDI location decisions.

NOTE

1. *The Wall Street Journal* (Tax Report, August 4, 1993, page 1, and Politics and Policy, August 19, 1993, page A12) has recently reported that controversy still surrounds California's unitary system. Barclays Bank has appealed to the Supreme Court to reject the unitary system. A spokesperson for Price Waterhouse commented that California's modified approach (water's edge unitary) did not appease all critics.

References

Allworth, Julian S. 1988. *The Finance, Investment and Taxation Decisions of Multinationals.* (New York: Basil Blackwell).

Altshuler, Rosanne, and Paolo Fulghieri. 1990. "Incentive Effects of Foreign Tax Credits on Multinationals." Columbia University, mimeo.

Amemiya, Takeshi. 1977. "On a Two-Step Estimation of a Multivariate Logit Model," *Journal of Econometrics* 8:13-21.

Arpan, Jeffrey S. and David A. Ricks. 1986. "Foreign Direct Investment in the U.S., 1974-1984," *International Business Studies* 17:149-153.

Auerbach, Alan J., and James R. Hines, Jr. 1988. "Investment Tax Incentives and Frequent Tax Reform," *American Economic Review* 78:211-16.

Balassa, Bela. 1986. "The Determinants of Intra-Industry Specialization in United States Trade," *Oxford Economic Papers* 38:220-233.

Bard, Yonathan. 1973. *Nonlinear Parameter Estimation.* New York: Academic Press.

Bartik, Timothy. 1985. "Business Location Decisions in the United States: Estimates of the Effects of Unionization, Taxes, and Other Characteristics of States," *Journal of Business and Economic Statistics* 3:14-22.

_____. 1991. *Who Benefits from State and Local Economic Development Policies?* Kalamazoo, MI: W.E. Upjohn Institute for Employment Research

Baumol, William, Sue Anne Betsy Blackman, and Edward N. Wolff. 1989. *Productivity and American Leadership: The Long View.* Cambridge, MA: MIT Press.

Bezirganian, Steve D. 1991. "U.S. Affiliates of Foreign Companies: Operations in 1989." *Survey of Current Business* 71, 7 (July):72-92.

Blackley, Paul, James R. Follain, Jr., and Jan Ondrich. 1984. "Box-Cox Estimation of Hedonic Models: How Serious is the Iterative OLS Variance Bias?" *Review of Economics and Statistics* 66:348-353.

Börsch-Supan, Axel. 1987. *Econometric Analysis of Discrete Choice.* Berlin: Springer-Verlag.

_____. 1990. "On the Compatibility of Nested Logit Models with Utility Maximization," *Journal of Econometrics* 43:373-88.

Boskin, Michael J., and William G. Gale. 1987. "New Results on the Effects of Tax Policy on the International Location of Investment." In *The Effects of Capital Taxation on Capital Accumulation*, Martin Feldstein, ed. Chicago: University of Chicago Press, pp. 201-222.

Box, G.E.P., and D.R. Cox, 1964. "An Analysis of Transformations." *Journal of the Royal Statistical Society*, Series B, 26:211-252.

Carlton, Dennis W. 1983. "The Location and Employment Choices of New Firms: An Econometric Model With Discrete and Continuous Endogenous Variables," *Review of Economics and Statistics* 65:440-449.

Carroll, Robert, and Michael Wasylenko. 1993. "Do State Business Climates Still Matter? Evidence of a Structural Change." Metropolitan Studies Program, Syracuse University, January.

Caves, Richard E. 1982. *Multinational Enterprise and Economics Analysis.* Cambridge, England: Cambridge University Press.

Chung, William K., and Gregory G. Fouch. 1983. "Foreign Direct Investment in The United States in 1982," *Survey of Current Business* 63, 8 (August):31-41.

Cole, Robert E., and Donald R. Deskins, Jr. 1988. "Racial Factors in Site Location and Employment Patterns of Japanese Auto Firms in America," *California Management Review* (Fall):9-22.

Coughlin, Cletus C., Joseph V. Terza, and Vachira Arromdee. 1991. "State Characteristics and the Location of Foreign Direct Investment within the United States," *Review of Economics and Statistics* 73:675-83.

Culem, Claudy G. 1988. "The Locational Determinants of Direct Investments Among Industrialized Countries," *European Economic Review* 32:885-904.

Curme, Michael A., Barry T. Hirsch, and David A. MacPherson. 1990. "Union Membership and Contract Coverage in the United States, 1983-1988," *Industrial and Labor Relations Review* 44:5-33.

Cushman, David O. 1987. "The Effects of Real Wages and Labor Productivity on Foreign Direct Investment," *Southern Economics Journal* 54:174-185.

Daly, Andrew J., and Stanley Zachary. 1978. "Improved Multiple Choice Models." In *Determinants of Travel Choice*, David Hensher and Quasim Dalvi, eds. Farmborough: Saxon House, pp. 335-57.

Davidson, William H. 1989. "The Location of Foreign Direct Investment Activity: Country Characteristics and Experience Effects," *International Business Studies* 11:9-22.

Debreu, Gerard. 1960. "Review of R. Luce, Individual Choice Behavior," *American Economic Review* 50:186-88.

DeLong, J. Bradford, and Lawrence H. Summers. 1991. "Equipment Investment and Economic Growth," *Quarterly Journal of Economics* 106:445-502.

Dooley, Michael, Jeffrey Frankel, and Donald J. Mathieson. 1987. "International Capital Mobility: What Do Saving-Investment Correlations Tell Us?" International Monetary Fund Staff Paper No. 34:503-530.

Dunning, John H. 1980. "Toward an Eclectic Theory of International Production," *Journal of International Business Studies* 11 (Spring/Summer):9-31.

Dunning, John H., ed. 1985. *Multinational Enterprises, Economic Structure and International Competitiveness.* New York: John Wiley & Sons.

The Economist. 1992. "World Economy Survey: Mysteries of the Modern" (September 19-25) p. 18-24.

Feldstein, Martin, ed. 1987. *The Effects of Taxation on Capital Accumulation.* Chicago: University of Chicago Press.

Feldstein, Martin, and Charles Horioka. 1980. "Domestic Saving and International Capital Flows," *Economic Journal* 90:314-329.

Feldstein, Martin, and Phillipe Bacchetta. 1991. "National Saving And International Investment." In *National Saving and Economic Performance,* B. Douglas Bernheim and John B. Shoven, eds. Chicago: University of Chicago Press, pp. 201-220.

Frankel, Jeffrey. 1992. "Measuring International Capital Mobility: A Review." *Proceedings of the American Economic Association* 82, 2:197-202.

Freeman, Richard B. and Mark H. Medoff. 1984. *What Do Unions Do?* New York: Basic Books.

Friedman, Joseph, Daniel Gerlowski, and Jonathan Silberman. 1989. "The Determinants of Foreign Plant Location across States." Temple University, mimeo.

Glickman, Norman J., and Douglas P. Woodward. 1987. "Regional Patterns of Foreign Direct Investment in the United States." Final Report prepared for the U.S. Department of Commerce, Economic Development Administration, Research and Evaluation Division.

_____. 1989. *The New Competitors: How Foreign Investors are Changing the U.S. Economy.* New York: Basic Books.

Goodspeed, Timothy J., and Daniel J. Frisch. 1989. "U.S. Tax Policy and the Overseas Activities of U.S. Multinational Corporations." Office of Tax Analysis, U.S. Department of Treasury, August 24, mimeo.

Gordon, Roger H., and Joosung Jun. 1992. "Taxes and the Form of Ownership of Foreign Corporate Equity." National Bureau of Economic Research Working Paper No. 4159.

Graham, Edward M., and Paul R. Krugman. 1991. *Foreign Direct Investment in the United States,* 2nd edition. Washington, DC: Institute for International Economics.

Hartman, David G. 1985. "Tax Policy and Foreign Direct Investment." *Journal of Public Economics* 26:107-121.

_____. 1984. "Tax Policy and Foreign Direct Investment in the United States," *National Tax Journal* 37:475-487.

Hausman, Jerry A. and David A. Wise. 1978. "A Conditional Probit Model for Qualitative Choice: Discrete Decisions Recognizing Interdependence and Heterogeneous Preferences," *Econometrica* 46:403-426.

Hellerstein, Jerome R. 1983. *State Taxation.* Boston, MA: Warrent, Gorham, and Lamont.

Helms, L. Jay. 1985. "The Effect of State and Local Taxes on Economic Growth: A Time Series-Cross Section Approach," *Review of Economics and Statistics* 67:574-582.

Hensher, David. 1986. "Sequential and Full Information Maximum Likelihood Estimation of a Nested Logit Model," *Review of Economics and Statistics* 68:657-67.

Hines, James R. Jr., 1988. "Multinational Transfer Pricing and Its Tax Consequences: Where the Profits Are." Princeton University mimeo, November.

Hines, James R. Jr., and R. Glenn Hubbard. 1989. "Coming Home to America: Dividend Repatriations by U.S. Multinationals." Paper presented at the National Bureau of Economic Research Conference on International Taxation, Nassau, Bahamas, February 24-25.

Hines, James R., Jr., and Eric M. Rice. 1990. "Fiscal Paradise: Foreign Tax Havens and American Business." Princeton University mimeo, April.

Horst, Thomas. 1977. "American Taxation of Multinational Firms." *American Economic Review* 67:376-389.

Howenstine, Ned. 1989. "U.S. Affiliates of Foreign Companies: 1987 Benchmark Survey Reslts," *Survey of Current Business* 89, 7 (July): 116-137.

Hufbauer, Gary Glyde. 1992. *United States Taxation of International Income: Blueprint for Reform.* Washington, DC: Institute for International Economics.

Hymer, Stephen H. 1976. *The International Operations of National Firms.* Cambridge, MA: MIT Press.

Joint Committee on Taxation. 1987. "General Explanation of the Tax Reform Act of 1986." H.R. 3838, 99th Congress, Public Law 99-514.

Jun, Joosung. 1989. "Tax Policy and International Direct Investment." National Bureau of Economic Research, Working Paper No. 3048.

_____. 1989. "U.S. Tax Policy and Direct Investment Abroad." National Bureau of Economic Research, Working Paper No. 3049.

Kahley, William. 1989. "U.S. and Foreign Direct Investment Patterns," *Economic Review, Federal Reserve Bank of Atlanta* (November/December):42-57.

Kitchen, Harry M. 1987. "Canada." In *Comparative Tax Systems: Europe, Canada, and Japan,* Joseph A. Pechman, ed. Arlington, VA: Tax Analysts, chapter 8.

Levinsohn, James. 1989. "The Determinants of Foreign Direct Investment in the United States, 1979-85: Comment." In *Trade Policies for International Competitiveness,* Robert C. Feenstra, ed. Chicago: University of Chicago Press, pp. 80-83.

Luger, Michael I., and Sudhir Shetty. 1985. "Determinants of Foreign Plant Start-Ups in the United States: Lessons for Policymakers in the Southeast," *Vanderbilt Journal of Transnational Law* (Spring): 223-45).

Maddala, G.S. 1986. *Limited Dependent and Qualitative Variables in Econometrics.* New York: Cambridge University Press.

Mann, Catherine L. 1989. "Determinants of Japanese Direct Investment in U.S. Manufacturing Industries." Washington, DC: Board of Governors of the Federal Reserve System International Finance Department Discussion Papers No. 362, September.

McLure, Charles. 1992. "Substituting Consumption-Based Direct Taxation for Income Taxes as the International Norm." *National Tax Journal* 45 (June):145-154.

McConnell, James E. 1980. "Foreign Direct Investment in the United States," *Annals of the Association of American Geographers* 70:259-270.

McFadden, Daniel. 1974. "Conditional Logit Analysis of Qualitative Choice Behavior." In *Frontiers in Econometrics*, P. Zarembka, ed. New York: Academic Press, pp. 105-142.

_____. 1978. "Modelling the Choice of Residential Location." In *Spatial Interaction Theory and Planning Models*, Anders Karlqvist, ed. New York: North-Holland, pp. 75-96.

Moore, Michael L., Bert M. Steece, and Charles W. Swenson. 1987. "An Analysis of the Impact of State Income Rates and Bases on Foreign Investment," *Accounting Review* 62 (October): 671-685.

New York State Department of Taxation and Finance, Office of Tax Policy Analysis. 1992. *Business Tax Analysis: The Taxation of Affiliated Groups.* Volume I: *Overview* (February).

Newlon, Timothy S. 1987. "Tax Policy and Multinational Firms' Financial Policy and Investment Decisions." Ph.D. dissertation, Princeton University.

Obstfeld, Maurice. 1986. *Capital Mobility in the World Economy: Theory and Measurement.* Carnegie-Rochester Conference Series on Public Policy. Amsterdam: North-Holland.

Ohuallachain, Breandan. 1984. "Linkages and Foreign Direct Investment," *Economic Geography* 60:238-253.

Pechman, Joseph A., ed. 1987. *Comparative Tax Systems: Europe, Canada, and Japan.* Arlington, VA: Tax Analysts.

Ray, Edward John. 1989. "The Determinants of Foreign Direct Investment in the United States." In *Trade Policies for International Competitiveness*, Robert C. Feenstra, ed. Chicago: University of Chicago Press, pp. 53-84.

Reich, Robert. 1990. "Who Is Us?" *Harvard Business Review* (January-February):53-64.

150

Scholl, Russell B. 1989. "The International Investment Position in 1988," *Survey of Current Business* 89 (June):41-49.

Scholl, Russell B., Raymond J. Mataloni, and Steve D. Bezirganian. 1992. "The International Investment Position of the United States in 1991." *Survey of Current Business* 72(6):46-59.

Shah, Anwar, and Joel Slemrod. 1990. "Tax Sensitivity of Foreign Direct Investment: An Empirical Assessment." World Bank County Economics Department Working Paper No. 434, June.

Sinn, Hans-Werner. 1990. "Taxation and the Birth of Foreign Subsidiaries." Princeton University, October, mimeo.

Slemrod, Joel. 1989. "Tax Effects on Foreign Direct Investment in the U.S.: Evidence from a Cross-Country Comparison." National Bureau of Economic Research, Working Paper No. 3042.

_____. 1990. "The Impact of the Tax Reform Act of 1986 on Foreign Direct Investment to and from the United States." National Bureau of Economic Research, Working Paper No. 3234.

Spitzer, John J., 1982. "A Primer on Box-Cox Estimation," *Review of Economics and Statistics* 64:307-313.

Tyson, Laura. 1992. *Who's Bashing Whom? Trade Conflict in High Technology Industries.* Washington, DC: Institute for International Economics.

U.S. Bureau of the Census. 1992. *Statistical Abstract of the United States: 1992,* 112 edition. Washington, DC.

U.S. Department of Commerce, Bureau of Economic Analysis. 1981. *Survey of Current Business* 61, 8 (August):42.

_____. 1983. *Survey of Current Business,* 63, 8 (August):31-32.

_____. 1985. *Survey of Current Business,* 65, 8 (August):47.

_____. 1988. *Survey of Current Business,* 68, 9 (August):69.

_____. 1988. "Foreign Direct Investment Position in the United States: Detail for Position and Balance of Payment Flows, 1987." *Survey of Current Business* 68, 8 (August):69-83.

_____. 1989. *Survey of Current Business,* 69(8) (August):47.

U.S. Department of Commerce, International Trade Administration. various issues. *Foreign Direct Investment in the United States.*

Wasylenko, Michael. 1984. "Disamenities, Local Taxation, and the Intrametropolitan Location of Households and Firms." In *The Changing Economic and Fiscal Structure,* Robert D. Ebel and T. Vernon Henderson, eds. Greenwich, CT: JAI Press, pp. 97-116.

_____. 1991. "Empirical Evidence on Interregional Business Location Decisions and the Role of Fiscal Incentives on Economic Development." In *Industry Location and Public Policy,* Henry W. Herzog, Jr. and Alan M. Schlottmann eds. Knoxville, TN: University of Tennessee Press.

Wasylenko, Michael and Therese McGuire. 1985. "Jobs and Taxes: The Effect of Business Climate on States' Employment Growth Rates," *National Tax Journal* 38 (December): 497-511.

Williams, Huw C.W.L. 1977. "On the Formation of Travel Demand Models and Economic Evaluation Measures of User Benefit," *Environment and Planning*, A9:285-344.

Williamson, Jeffrey G. 1991. "Productivity and American Leadership: A Review," *Journal of Economic Literature* 29:51-68.

Woodward, Douglas. 1991. "Locational Determinants of Japanese Manufacturing Start-ups in the United States." University of South Carolina at Columbia, mimeo.

_____. 1992. "Locational Determinants of Japanese Manufacturing Start-Ups in the United States," *Southern Economic Journal* 58: 690-708.

Young, Kan H. 1988. "The Effects of Taxes and Rates of Return on Foreign Direct Investment in the United States," *National Tax Journal* 41:109-121.

Index

Acquisitions and mergers, 27
Affiliates, foreign
  state definitions of, 23
  wage levels of employees, 136
Agglomeration economies
  in domestic firm decisions, 62
  in location choice analysis, 79
  when not attractive to foreign firms,
    140–41
  See also Employment
Arromdee, Vachira, 57t, 58
Asset values
  of foreign direct investment in United
    States, 7–9, 135
  portfolio, 5–7
  of U.S. plants, 33
Attractions
  agglomeration economies, 58, 59, 62,
    134, 140
  industry group concentration, 140
  labor pool, skilled, 140
  market demand measures, 58
  urbanization economies as, 58
  See also Industry groups

Bacchetta, Phillipe, 13
Bartik, Timothy, 59, 62, 134
Bezirganian, Steve D., 1, 6t, 9t
Börsch-Supan, Axel, 71, 112
Boskin, Michael, 49, 50t
Box, G. E. P., 107
Box-Cox regressions, 107–9

California
  foreign manufacturing plants in, 40
  new plant investment in, 45, 47–48,
    138
Canada
  FDI asset values in United States, 7–9,
    135
  firms in United States from, 27, 40, 42,
    45, 137

Capital
  costs as determinant of FDI, 10
  taxation effect on mobility, 14–19
  tax systems across countries to
    allocate, 15–16
Capital flows
  controls as barriers to, 14
  within European Community, 13
  factors influencing mobility of, 12–14
  response to taxation differences, 14–15
Capital-import neutral tax system, 17,
    20, 49
Capital-export neutral (CEN) concept
  conditions when not applied, 21
  incentives to invest overseas, 20
  tax systems using, 15–16
  territorial tax systems, 17
Capital stock (of FDI in United States),
    5–9, 135
Carroll, Robert, 62
Caves, Richard, 16, 21, 54
CEN. *See* Capital-export neutral (CEN)
  concept
Chemicals and Allied Products
  attraction of foreign firms to certain
    states, 140
  new foreign plants, 45, 47–48, 138
  wages in, 136
Chung, William K., 9t
Cole, Robert E., 59
Comparative advantage, state, 141
Competition
  among states for foreign investors,
    122, 126
  from foreign firms, 141
Competitive advantage
  creation of, 10
  in industrial organization theory of
    FDI, 11
Connecticut (new plant investment), 45,
    47–48, 138
Corporate income tax
  as deterrent to FDI, 141–42

About the Institute

The W.E. Upjohn Institute for Employment Research is a nonprofit research organization devoted to finding and promoting solutions to employment-related problems at the national, state, and local level. It is an activity of the W.E. Upjohn Unemployment Trustee Corporation, which was established in 1932 to administer a fund set aside by the late Dr. W.E. Upjohn, founder of The Upjohn Company, to seek ways to counteract the loss of employment income during economic downturns.

The Institute is funded largely by income from the W.E. Upjohn Unemployment Trust, supplemented by outside grants, contracts, and sales of publications. Activities of the Institute are comprised of the following elements: (1) a research program conducted by a resident staff of professional social scientists; (2) a competitive grant program, which expands and complements the internal research program by providing financial support to researchers outside the Institute; (3) a publications program, which provides the major vehicle for the dissemination of research by staff and grantees, as well as other selected work in the field; and (4) an Employment Management Services division, which manages most of the publicly funded employment and training programs in the local area.

The broad objectives of the Institute's research, grant, and publication programs are to: (1) promote scholarship and experimentation on issues of public and private employment and unemployment policy; and (2) make knowledge and scholarship relevant and useful to policymakers in their pursuit of solutions to employment and unemployment problems.

Current areas of concentration for these programs include: causes, consequences, and measures to alleviate unemployment; social insurance and income maintenance programs; compensation; workforce quality; work arrangements; family labor issues; labor-management relations; and regional economic development and local labor markets.